Praise for The Innovation Workout

'Read The Innovation Workout and your innovation muscles will be bulging. Full of no-nonsense practical advice, handy checklists and definitions, this book is written in a refreshingly accessible and jargon-free way. It will help anyone charged with innovating in organisations large and small.'

David Simoes-Brown, Co-Founder, 100%Open

'A practical and thought-provoking guide laced with interesting real life examples, this book will really help people incorporate innovation into their workplace.'

Fiona Gibson, Investment and Corporate Finance Executive, Leading UK Bank

'Practical, insightful, and easy to apply. This book is packed full of the secrets you'll need to take ideas from concepts to fully developed products!'

Alison Paul, New Product Development Manager, Bupa UK

The Innovation Workout

The Innovation Workout

The 10 tried-and-tested steps that will build your creativity and innovation skills

Lucy Gower

PEARSON

Harlow, England • London • New York • Boston • San Francisco • Toronto • Sydney
Auckland • Singapore • Hong Kong • Tokyo • Seoul • Taipei • New Delhi
Cape Town • São Paulo • Mexico City • Madrid • Amsterdam • Munich • Paris • Milan

Pearson Education Limited
Edinburgh Gate
Harlow CM20 2JE
United Kingdom
Tel: +44 (0)1279 623623
Web: www.pearson.com/uk

First published 2015 (print and electronic)

© Pearson Education Limited 2015 (print and electronic)

The right of Lucy Gower to be identified as author of this work has been asserted by her in accordance with the Copyright, Designs and Patents Act 1988.

Pearson Education is not responsible for the content of third-party internet sites.

ISBN: 978–1-292–08501–2 (print)
 978–1-292–08503–6 (PDF)
 978–1-292–08504-3 (ePub)
 978–1-292–08502–9 (eText)

British Library Cataloguing-in-Publication Data
A catalogue record for the print edition is available from the British Library

Library of Congress Cataloging-in-Publication Data
Gower, Lucy, author.
 The innovation workout / Lucy Gower.
 pages cm. — (The business gym)
 Includes index.
 ISBN 978-1-292-08501-2 (pbk.)
 1. Creative ability in business. 2. Creative thinking. 3. Technological innovations.
  4. New products. I. Title.
 HD53.G69 2015
 650.1—dc23

 2015026653

10 9 8 7 6 5 4 3 2 1
19 18 17 16 15

Cover design by Two Associates
Print edition typeset in 10/13 Scene Std by 71
Print edition printed in Great Britain by Henry Ling Ltd, at the Dorset Press, Dorchester, Dorset

NOTE THAT ANY PAGE CROSS REFERENCES REFER TO THE PRINT EDITION

Contents

Get your innovation off to the right start by thinking
big to understand your problem or unmet need and
articulate it in a way that inspires others to get involved.

Learn techniques to better understand your customers,
to enable you to develop innovations that meet their
needs.

Get to grips with what is happening in your market
today and spot trends to help develop innovation for
the future.

Contents

About the author

 Lucy Gower is an innovation specialist. She is a freelance trainer, coach and consultant. She established the first innovation programme at the NSPCC, one of the UK's largest children's charities, in 2007. Since 2012 she has worked with a range of organisations in the charity and corporate sectors, both in the UK and overseas, to help them develop their strategy people and operational approach to innovation. Clients include 100%Open, Amnesty International, Cystic Fibrosis Trust, The Institute of Fundraising, Nesta, nfpSynergy, Oxfam and The Children's Society.

Contact Lucy at:

Website: **www.lucidity.org.uk**
Email: **lucy@lucidity.org.uk**
Twitter: **@lucyinnovation**

Author's acknowledgements

With thanks to Phil Barden, Simon Berry, Steve Bridger, Mark Brill, Robert Burns, Mark Champkins, Helen Coyle, Ben Davies, Bob Francis, Jon Gower, Jude Habib, Anne McCrossan, Martin Hills, Lydia Messling, Sean Miller, Stephen George, Andy Hamflett, Roland Harwood, Chris Parker, Jacob Rolin, Steve Rowe, David Simoes-Brown, Murray Sim, Pierre Swart, David Townson, Richard Turner, Karl Wilding and Rob Woods.

Twitter community including @iramey @grahamguy @annkempster @tweetsfromlily @raymundf23 @darrin_johnson @innovateDevelop @London_Lady @_ieuan @mattsagaser @Beth_Upton @benatrodd @Tamsin_Tweets @fellowcreative @joelvoysey @LydiaRagoonanan @NickSherrard @EllenJanssens @vkp67 @jamiepither @adamcranfield @j_rehm @adriansalmon @mrs_gibb @GeorgeJulian @JPROSSER2 @HarveyJWade @IoFScotland @karlwilding @colalife @stevebridger @sounddelivery

Publisher's acknowledgements

We are grateful to the following for permission to reproduce copyright material:

Figures

Figure on page 112 reprinted with the permission of Free Press, a Division of Simon & Schuster, Inc., from DIFFUSION OF INNOVATIONS, 5E by Everett M. Rodgers. Copyright © 1995, 2003 by Everett M. Rogers. Copyright © 1962, 1971, 1983, by Free Press, A Division of Simon & Schuster, Inc. All rights reserved.

Picture Credits

The publisher would like to thank the following for their kind permission to reproduce their photographs:

(Key: b-bottom; c-centre; l-left; r-right; t-top)

Alamy Images: Jeffrey Blackler 65b, Maskot 44, Alison Thompson 52t; **Colalife:** Simon Berry 52b; **Daimler AG:** 50; **Dr Zaana Howard:** 89; **Image by Kallirroi Pouliadou:** In collaboration with Kevin Gaunt, Migle Padegimaite and Emily Keller, working on platooning and the future of automation in truck driving. 91; **innocent ltd:** 180; **Interface:** 65t; **Newsquest Somerset:** Steve Richardson 64; **Shutterstock.com**: Giideon 45t, mimagephotography 45b

All other images © Pearson Education

Every effort has been made to trace the copyright holders and we apologise in advance for any unintentional omissions. We would be pleased to insert the appropriate acknowledgement in any subsequent edition of this publication.

In some instances we have been unable to trace the owners of copyright material, and we would appreciate any information that would enable us to do so.

Introduction

Would you like to be more creative? Or perhaps you already have lots of creative ideas but find it hard to choose which ones to develop? Would you like to have more confidence about the quality of your ideas? Maybe you would like to inspire your colleagues and your boss with your smart thinking? Or would you like practical steps on how to turn your idea from a scribble on the back of an envelope into reality?

If you answered yes to any one of these questions, then *The Innovation Workout* can help you.

The Innovation Workout is a practical book designed to give you the confidence and tools to succeed at innovation, from improving your creativity, to generating lots of ideas, as well as choosing the best ideas, developing them and making them real.

How to get the most from *The Innovation Workout*

The workout takes you through every step of an innovation process. You can read *The Innovation Workout* from cover to cover, or just dip in and out of the sections that will help you most. Depending on your job role and current skills, you might not need all the steps right now, but reading them all will give you a solid background on the whole innovation process and help you appreciate how the parts that you contribute to are vital to the bigger picture.

There are practical exercises that you can apply to your everyday work, as well as a section with tips to help you tackle the most common innovation challenges. There is space to jot down your ideas and to record your progress.

You'll notice three icons highlighting either an Activity, what we regard as a Key idea or Media. The icons we will use are:

Activity　　**Key idea**　　**Media**

The Media icon indicates where you can also go online to **www .thebusinessgym.net** where you will find additional innovation resources including an innovation toolkit and templates to help you work through the different parts of the innovation process as well as inspiration from successful innovators.

If you are working on something right now you can use this workout to take you through your live project, or to help you if you have got stuck at a particular point. Even with a live project it might be that not all the stages will apply to you (innovation is a bit like that because it is not strictly a linear process and no two ideas are exactly the same), but you can still dip in and out of the steps that apply. If you are not working on something specific you can still learn about innovation or apply some of the tips to inspire your day-to-day work.

Being a brilliant innovator requires a range of skills including being able to sniff out an opportunity, thinking creatively to solve problems, developing and refining the ideas with the most potential, being able to inspire and influence others, tenacity and resilience to persevere when your idea does not work first time, as well as flexibility and humility to learn and adapt in order to make your idea happen.

The way to learn and build your innovation confidence is by doing. Reading the theory is very different from experiencing, especially with innovation because as you step out of your comfort zone there is often a feeling of discomfort as you explore the unknown. The more of the exercises you do, the more discomfort you will experience and the more proficient and confident you will become!

The first step on **page xix** is a self-assessment to help you identify your current innovation skills and where your strengths and weaknesses are so you can focus on the areas that you want to improve on.

After reading *The Innovation Workout* and working through the exercises, take the self-assessment again to see how you have progressed and reflect on your learning, improved skills and confidence as well as areas that you would like to work on some more.

Finally, there is a section to help you put your skills into action, with guidance on finding a mentor to support you, and tips on how to work with them to achieve your goals.

Self-assessment questionnaire

Complete this questionnaire before you begin *The Innovation Workout* to gain a quick understanding and overview of your current innovation confidence and skills. Don't think too hard about your answers. There is no right answer, just complete it quickly using your gut instinct.

Score yourself on a scale of 1 to 10, with 10 indicating a high level of confidence and skill and 1 the lowest.

1. I am confident at identifying the root cause of a problem.

2. I am creative.

3. I can easily come up with multiple solutions to problems.

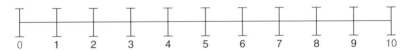

4. I am excellent at making my ideas happen.

5. I have large and diverse networks.

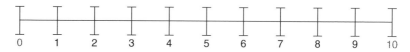

6. I know how to develop my ideas.

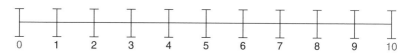

7. I can easily decide where to focus to make the most difference.

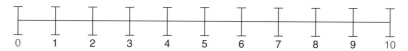

8. I am quick to spot potential opportunities.

9. I am flexible to adapt or change my plans if situations change.

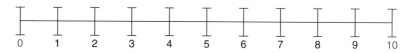

10. I have a good understanding of my customers and the marketplace.

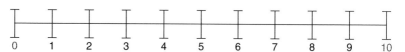

11. I am comfortable with challenging the status quo.

12. I regularly step outside my comfort zone and try new things.

13. I happily admit my mistakes in order that I, and others, learn from them.

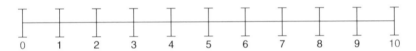

14. I am comfortable asking others for help and advice.

15. I am a great listener.

16. I feel equipped to influence and inspire others to get on board with my ideas.

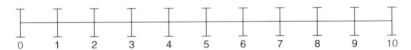

17. I am confident in developing strategic business models.

18. I am objective in making strategic decisions about both progressing and stopping ideas.

19. I do what I believe to be right, even if others criticise me for it.

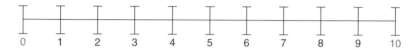

20. I am willing to take risks and go the extra mile to achieve better results.

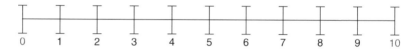

My overall innovation score is . . . .

Once you have read the book, completed all the exercises and spent some time with your mentor, do this questionnaire again (on **page 205**) and notice which areas you have developed in and which still require attention.

So, if you are ready, let's get some things agreed up front.

What is innovation?

Over the last few years it seems that everyone is talking about innovation. It's become part of marketing slogans, often with no substance, at the top of the corporate buzzword charts. I've seen it used indiscriminately to make practically anything sound more sexy or interesting than it actually is, from political policies to mortgage deals and even a new flavour of soup. So before we begin flexing our innovation muscles let's be really clear on what innovation means.

The Oxford English Dictionary describes innovation as:

- the action or process of innovating;
- a new method, idea, product, etc.

In addition innovation is not about making *any* idea happen, it's about taking action to make the good ideas happen that get you or your organisation closer to achieving a goal, for example developing new products that customers want or a process that makes employees' or customers' lives easier, or a system that helps the organisation operate more effectively. If an idea is new to your organisation, even if it has been done elsewhere, it still counts as innovation.

Big ideas and small changes

There are two key approaches to innovation.

1. Disruptive innovation

This is the quest for the illusive 'next big thing', the idea that will change or disrupt the way your business (or all businesses!) works. There are not so many of these next big things. The invention of the World Wide Web is an example of a disruptive innovation that changed how we communicate and how we make purchases across every business in the world. Disruptive innovation takes time and resources and comes with a high degree of risk, but also great rewards if you can successfully disrupt and be the leader in the new disrupted marketplace.

2. Incremental innovation

This involves the patient and relentless pursuit of improvement by making small changes that add up to make a big difference. For example, the GB cycling team had an incremental innovation strategy for the 2012 Olympic Games. They made hundreds of small improvements to their equipment, training, lifestyle and diets that combined to help them achieve their mission of winning gold. The GB cycling team won 12 medals, 8 of which were gold, using this incremental innovation strategy. We can all make small changes to our day-to-day work and lives that can add up to make a big difference in achieving both our personal and professional goals.

The two approaches are not mutually exclusive. You can choose to develop incremental innovation while at the same time seeking to disrupt and find the next big thing.

Why is innovation important?

Whatever job you do or industry you work in, the development of new technologies is changing your work as well as your personal life. For example, access to social media has changed the way we communicate with customers, colleagues, friends and family. How we make buying decisions has also changed.

What do you do when you are thinking about buying something?

Most people ask their friends for product recommendations and then also look for recommendations online. People trust other people for recommendations more than advertisements, making the value of customer endorsement on websites like Amazon and TripAdvisor priceless.

Organisations have to respond to change by innovating if they are going to survive. Organisations that do not innovate run the very real risk of going out of business. Consider Kodak, which despite patenting digital photography in the 1970s failed to respond to the massive market trend for digital photography, which eventually put the company out of business in January 2012.

What does innovation mean for you?

It is not just organisations that must innovate to survive in a fast-changing world. It applies to you too.

The pace of technological developments is not going to slow down any time soon. This means that the things you take for granted today – your job, the skills you need, the lifestyle you lead – will change over the next few years. In fact you can probably think of some of these changes you have already experienced in just the last ten years.

Many of the most popular jobs in 2014, including 'digital marketer' and 'app developer', didn't even exist ten years ago and the skills needed today to do these new jobs continue to change too. This means that to thrive, you too must change. You too have to be able to understand the environment that you live and work in, spot opportunities and constantly adapt.

For you, perfecting your skills in innovation is an opportunity that has the potential to open up vast possibilities. Innovation is not something that should be confined to your day-to-day work environment; you can apply the skills to every aspect of your life. Learning to solve problems and then exploring creative solutions that you can then put into action, can reap rewards and help you achieve your ambitions both professionally and personally.

Part 1

10 steps to enhance your innovation skills

Step 1   Pinpoint your purpose

Step 2   Know and understand your customers

Step 3   Your market today and predicting the trends of tomorrow

Step 4   Build your creative capacity

Step 5   Creative superstardom and lots of ideas

Step 6   Don't expect anyone else to like your idea

Step 7   Filter and choose the best ideas

Step 8   Prototype, fail fast and refine

Step 9   Pilot, adapt and invest

Step 10   Take your ideas to market

Step 1

Pinpoint your purpose

After reading this step you will learn how to:

- Confidently start your innovation by picking areas that have the potential to make the most impact

- Describe the problem that you are setting out to solve, or the unmet need that you are addressing, in a way that other people can easily understand

- Have absolute clarity on why your innovation is important and be able to communicate that in a way that inspires others to get involved.

'If I had one hour to save the world, I would spend fifty-five minutes defining the problem and only five minutes finding the solution.'

Albert Einstein (allegedly), Nobel Prize in Physics

Clarity on what you are innovating for is the first secret of successful innovation. Time taken at the beginning of the process to identify the areas that matter to you, your organisation or your customers will massively increase your chances of innovation success.

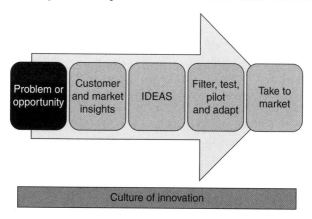

Steps for successful innovation

Innovation is not about making *any* idea happen, it's about making the ideas happen that get you or your organisation closer to achieving its goal. All good innovation must have a purpose. It must do *at least* one of the following:

- Address an unmet need: for example, the online startup Airbnb, which allows people like you and me to rent out part of their property to others, met the need for choice of affordable accommodation around the world.

- Solve a problem: like Australia's V/Line trains, 'Guilt Trips' offering off-peak tickets to help parents encourage their kids to visit them.

- Exploit an opportunity: 'The Facebook', a website originally developed in 2004 to connect Harvard students, was overwhelmed with demand. By December 2014 Facebook had 1.35 billion monthly active users.

- Provide a better, more effective way to do something: for example, 'ode', a device that encourages appetite in people with dementia, helping them stay healthy and live independently for longer.

- Help you achieve your goal or mission: for example, the development of the contraceptive pill achieved Margaret Sanger's goal to give women the right to control their bodies.

 You can read more about the above innovations at:

www.thebusinessgym.net

Sometimes it can feel frustrating; when you have a brilliant idea, you just want to get on with it. Successful innovators have the discipline to go back to basics and check that their innovation does meet one of the above criteria. If you start innovating without defining why first, you will struggle to succeed later in the process.

Your problem might be about how to better address your customer needs, in which case you might have to find out more about your customers first. **(See Step 2 for help on how to do this.)**

What if innovation happens by accident?

There are many examples when innovation has happened by accident. One of the most famous stories is that of the *Post-It®Note*. In an attempt to develop super strong adhesives for the aerospace industry, 3M failed and accidently produced weak glue that it shelved. It was quite literally put on a shelf, until years later Art Fry, a product development engineer, discovered it was excellent for sticking his page markers in his hymn book to stop them falling out and losing his place. Problem solved. Good innovations, even if they happen by accident, still solve a problem or meet an unmet need. *Post-it Notes* are now used by customers in all sorts of ways and are sold in over 150 countries.

Don't rush to solutions

We have a tendency to jump to solutions. We learn at school to find solutions, we get rewarded for getting things right. When we join the workforce we follow set plans and work to objectives or key performance indicators (KPIs) that are predefined. How many times have you been asked to be solution focused? In many organisations there is little room to challenge plans or how things are done and explore whether there is a better way than the current solution. This can mean that under pressure to perform fast, we jump to solutions too quickly, without taking time to understand the real root of the problem or the thing we are innovating around. If you don't spend some time at the beginning of your innovation process to really understand and articulate why the innovation is important you could waste time, energy and resources solving the wrong problem.

Case study

Solving the wrong problem

In the early 1970s, Procter & Gamble's (P&G's) marketers were competing with Colgate-Palmolive's new soap product, *Irish Spring,* which had a distinctive green stripe and a promise of 'refreshment'.

P&G was copying the green stripe and testing its own versions of the soap to compete with *Irish Spring.* None of the P&G products was matching up. The company couldn't make a better green-stripe bar.

But that was the point. They were trying to solve the wrong problem. Once they took some time to unpick the real problem they realised that the question wasn't 'How can we make a better green-stripe bar?' It was 'How might we create a more refreshing soap?' This reframing freed up the team to think more broadly and their creative ideas converged on the theme of finding refreshment from the sea, from which they developed a successful product called *Coast* – with blue and white stripes.

P&G was so focused on the green-striped soap that it missed the real problem. To be successful it had to look at the situation differently – from the customer's point of view. The customer wasn't looking for the best green stripy soap bar, they wanted the product that was going to make them feel the most refreshed.

Source: Berger, W. (2012). The secret phrase top innovators use. *Harvard Business Review* [online]. Available at: <https://hbr.org/2012/09/the-secret-phrase-top-innovato/>

Always remember that **innovation = problem × solution(s)**[1] – and for any problem there are many solutions. The innovator's talent is picking the best one.

Thinking big – be clear on the 'why?'

There are several tactics that you can use to help ensure you start innovating confidently with real purpose.

Ask 'Why?' ×5

At the start of any innovation project or idea, really challenge yourself and your colleagues to make sure you are absolutely certain of why it is important. Ask 'Why?' at least five times. Here is an example from a courier company to help you:

Initial problem Packages were delivered to the wrong address on more than one occasion.

Why? Because the person packing and dispatching them for delivery was in a hurry and dealing with customers at the same time. (Symptom)

Why? Because she's quite new to the dispatch part of the role and has not received training yet. (Symptom)

Why? Because the person who used to do dispatch had left. There is no checklist or instructions on how to do the job and everyone else was busy. (Symptom)

Why? Because there's been no time for training or writing procedures. (Symptom)

Why? Because there is no one in charge of effective training or putting basic procedures in place. (Root cause)

The problem wasn't about the packages being sent to the wrong address as it initially appeared. The *root cause* of the problem was the lack of leadership to develop a process or procedure.

Try using the '5 Whys?' technique on a problem that you are working on to check you are addressing the root cause and not just the symptom.

[1]nonon, no-nonsense innovation. Available at: <http://www.nonon.co.uk/>

My problem is ... _____

Why? Because ... _____
Why? Because ... _____
Why? Because ... _____
Why? Because ... _____
Why? Because ... _____

The root cause of the problem is ... _____

Chunking

Another tactic that can help you clarify why your innovation matters, is called chunking. I know it sounds a bit odd, but it works!

Are you a big picture thinker? Do you prefer to think about the overview of an issue? Or are you more comfortable getting stuck right into the detail of something?

We all have preferences, and no way of thinking is better than another, but when trying to identify the root cause of a problem it helps to chunk.

Chunking is a technique that helps you to think in different levels of detail. The basic way to move between big picture and detail is with two questions. To chunk up to the big picture view you ask 'Why?' and to chunk down into the detail you ask 'How?'

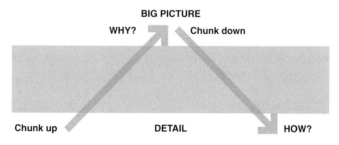

Chunk up and think big

You use 'chunking up' questions when you or your colleagues are immersed in the detail of a problem. For example, the detail of sending a direct mail to 10,000 customers involves decisions about the cost and thickness of the paper for the envelope. When you are immersed in the detail it is helpful to 'chunk up' to the bigger picture. Why are you sending it in the first place? What is the outcome you want? Chunking up helps you to think more strategically about the purpose of the task, and clarifies the problem you are solving.

Questions to ask to help you to 'chunk up' to the big picture

- Why?
- For what purpose?
- What are we trying to achieve here?
- What's important about this?
- What does success look like?
- What does this mean?

Chunking up to the big picture can also help drive creativity. Google's mission is to organise the world's information and make it universally accessible and useful. Apple didn't set out to make the next version of a Walkman by making improvements to the current Walkman model, it chunked right up to the ultimate purpose which was to enable customers to have 1,000 songs in their pocket. The iPod was developed from this big picture starting point.

Using the above as an example, think of a problem that you are working on. What questions can you ask to chunk up to think big?

What big picture thinking possibilities did you explore?

 For more on chunking up and chunking down go to page 5 of the innovation toolkit. at:

www.thebusinessgym.net

Ask provocative questions

Asking provocative questions can also help you to uncover the core purpose for your innovation and give you a steer on what you should be working on. They help you to think differently about an issue. Some examples of provocative questions are:

- What are our competitors working on that might put us out of business?
- What new technology might make our product obsolete tomorrow?
- What new legislation could potentially ruin our business?
- How might we run our business without staff?
- How might we give our products away for free and generate income?
- How might we communicate with our customers if we didn't use email?
- What if you had a limitless budget?
- What if you had no budget?

What are you currently working on? What provocative question can you ask to help you think differently and identify the areas to innovate around?

Communicate with confidence

When you are clear on your purpose, there are ways of articulating it that will help spark ideas and inspire others to get involved. One way of doing this is to frame your purposeful innovation as a question and ask 'How might we ... ?'

Warren Berger, in his *Harvard Business Review* blog,[2] explains how some of the most successful companies in business are known for tackling difficult creative challenges by first asking: How might we improve X ... or completely re-imagine Y ... or find a new way to accomplish Z?

Berger explains that when people try to innovate, they often talk about the challenges or the problems they are facing by using

[2]Berger, W. (2012). The secret phrase top innovators use. *Harvard Business Review*, [online] Available at: <https://hbr.org/2012/09/the-secret-phrase-top-innovato/>

language that can inhibit creativity instead of encouraging it. People often ask 'How *can* we do this?' or 'How *should* we do that?' The 'can' and 'should' in the question imply judgement. Can we really do it? Should we? Using the word 'might' instead of 'can' or 'should' defers judgement which releases people to create more options and therefore more possibilities for creativity. The use of the word 'might' also takes the pressure off coming up with something immediately workable. It subtly indicates that the idea you are suggesting might work or it might not, and either way that is ok, because we are just generating ideas about the possibilities.

Framing your innovation like this can be applied to almost anything. And learning how to frame your question will help you to get the best out of people. Your question needs to address the problem. It needs to be ambitious enough to provide opportunities for change and creativity, yet focused enough to be achievable. For example, 'How might we end world poverty?' is too big, but 'How might we ensure that every family in the UK has a safe place to live?' still has ambition, yet feels more achievable.

Like any new skill, framing the problem in the way to get the best results takes practice, but if you are spending time really considering the problem and articulating it well, you will be leagues ahead of many of your competitors.

Consider your innovation topic, or a problem that you are currently working on. How can you frame your question as a 'How might we?'

In this step about pinpointing your purpose, the essential innovation principles to remember are:

- Whatever sort of innovation you plan to do, you must be absolutely clear on the 'Why?' from the start.
- Innovation = problem × solution(s). Your innovation must meet an unmet need, solve a problem, exploit an opportunity, make something better or help you achieve a goal.
- To be absolutely clear on why your innovation is important, ask 'Why?' five times, chunk up or ask provocative questions.
- Articulate your innovation topic by framing it as a question and asking 'How might we . . . ?'

If you are reading this book from step to step, before you move on to **Step 2** make sure you can articulate what you are going to innovate around as a question.

Call to action

- Frame your problem as an interesting question, starting with 'How might we ... ?'
- Explain in one sentence why it's important to tackle this problem, starting with, 'It is important because ...'

  _____

  _____

- If you could take one idea from this step to practise in your day-to-day work, what would it be?

  _____

  _____

  _____

Step 2

Know and understand your customers

After reading this step you will learn how to:

- Get to grips with why it's important to first identify who your customer is and then understand what makes them tick

- Understand that when we talk about customers we could mean people who buy your products or services, your partners, internal customers, co-workers or other teams

- Use some tactics to find out more about your customers and how you can turn your knowledge into insight that you can use for your innovation.

'You never really understand a person until you consider things from his point of view.'

Harper Lee, author

The story so far

In **Step 1** you learned about taking a step back and making sure that you are absolutely clear on the purpose of your innovation, can tell others why it is important and frame it as a question that starts 'How might we . . . ?'

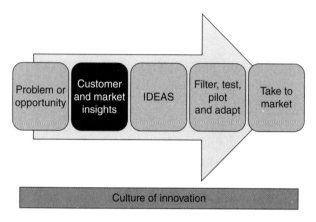

Steps for successful innovation

Why do you need to know about your customers?

The more you know about your customers and the more you seek to understand their needs, the greater your ability to develop products and services that they want or need. Developing innovation without understanding your customer is high risk – you are essentially taking a stab in the dark.

Who are your customers?

Think about the area you are innovating around and note down who your customers are – they might be internal teams, colleagues or specific groups of the general public. You can't focus on all of 'the general public' because it is too large and well, general. Think about a specific group. For example, a customer group or segment that one of my clients is working hard to understand consists of women who are considering going back to work after having children.

My customer group is _____

How can you get to know your customers?

One way to find out more about your customers is to ask them their opinions.

Focus groups: you can hold focus groups to find out views and attitudes to a particular topic, product or service. It is advisable, unless you have the skills in-house, to brief a market research agency to help you recruit your customer, group and construct questions that will answer the brief as well as facilitate the groups to get the most out of the participants. Often focus groups are more valuable in validating ideas further along in the process as described on **page 92.**

Survey: you can ask people for their views and opinions in a survey or a poll. It's simple to set up an online survey to email to your customers. You can also use social media channels to ask people what they think of issues and campaigns. Or you might choose to survey people face to face.

 Tips for writing surveys on online content are at:

www.thebusinessgym.net

Health warning*

'If I had asked my customers what they wanted, they would have said a faster horse.'

Attributed to Henry Ford

Asking people for their opinions and views comes with a health warning: people will often tell you what they want you to believe, or what they want to believe about themselves. For example, when asked about their charitable donations, they are more likely to say *'Yes I give regularly to several charities'* than admit to being uncharitable. Alternatively, they might tell you what they think you want to hear, for example *'I love this chocolate teapot idea'* to the hard-working entrepreneur setting up the flawed Chocolate

Teapot Start-up Corporation. With some products you can test what people tell you they would like with their actual behaviour. For example, when Google asked people about optimal search terms, they said they would like 30 search results to a page, but that slowed the search down. The optimum number of search terms according to the analytics was 10.

With this in mind there are plenty more ways that you can find out more about your customer needs and wants without asking them directly and this could provide you with more reliable inspiration for your innovation.

Become an innovation ethnographer

In an attempt to get to *really* know their customers many organisations are now using ethnography: the systematic study of people and cultures. Developed from the discipline of anthropology, researchers spend quality time with the group they are interested in, ideally over sustained periods of time, to observe and learn from their behaviours in their 'natural' habitat. There is also a part of ethnography known as netnography that looks at online behaviours.

Tesco led the way in understanding customer behaviour back in the 1990s with the Tesco Clubcard. The Clubcard was the first time a supermarket had really utilised understanding customer buying habits to develop new product offerings and bespoke offers based on customers' previous buying data.

Today, in addition to responding to customers' needs based on purchasing data, Tesco head office staff spend time with customers. They all do a stint in store, based on the premise that spending time understanding customers is critical to future business success.

Starbucks has been applying ethnography principles since 2002, relying on its army of baristas to share customer insights that feed into its innovation and product development process. The company also sends its teams on 'inspiration' field trips to other Starbucks stores to understand customers and trends across different countries and cultures.

Another example is a group of executives at a UK bread and baker supplier who experienced their customers by having breakfasts with them. It was apparently uncomfortable at first, but observing how their products were used provided much more insight than asking families to answer questions in a focus group and resulted in better products and happier customers.

Build more interactions with your customers every day

Make opportunities in day-to-day work to interact more with your customers. This helps to build a more complete picture, to help your innovation. Below are some suggestions.

Create conversations

Pick up the phone rather than emailing when you can, look for opportunities for dialogue, have face-to-face meetings. It is often the exchanges that come up in conversation that provide the best insights.

Consider complaints

What do your customers complain about? Listen in on customer service calls, follow conversations on social media, read and respond to complaint emails and letters (*especially* if customer care is not in your remit). Are there themes or recurring problems that indicate that something broader could be solved?

Ask more questions

Whenever you get the opportunity, ask more questions. Don't accept that the current product or process is the best way. You will gain lots from open questions, like:

- Tell me how you feel about that.
- What happened?
- Can you help me understand . . . ?

Practise listening

To get the most value from asking open questions, you have to listen. It sounds obvious, but it is a skill, like any other that you have to practise.

Collect data

Collect data about your customers and ensure your database is as accurate as it can be, include survey respondents, campaign evaluations and web analytics, and observe online chat rooms.

I expect you already do a lot of this work with customers. You may even have a team that specialises in information and insight for you. Either way, the good news is that it's not just down to you. Get as many people as you can on board to help you listen, observe and gather information. Then if you can also find a way to share that insight, for example in team meetings, via an insightful email or a notice board where you physically attach notices, then you really start to get a comprehensive picture of your customers.

Oh but there's a spanner in the works

The second health warning in this step is not to assume that customers will always know what they want or need. Many innovations provide solutions customers don't even know they need. This is where ethnography techniques can be really valuable. There are three things that you can look for that will help you identify what your customers or potential customers don't know.

1. **Look for what the customer needs but can't articulate.** Taking a photo of yourself, a 'selfie', has become increasingly popular. Because of this most smartphones now have a setting so you can see yourself on the screen which eliminates guesswork selfies featuring blurry half-cropped faces. With the framing problem solved then followed the realisation that most people's arms were not long enough to take a great selfie. The solution is the selfie stick, a retractable stick that attaches to your camera allowing you to get enough distance to take the perfect shot. Selfie takers were not demanding the selfie stick, or longer arms; someone spotted the need and made the product.

2. **Look for workarounds.** People make up for the limitations of existing solutions. Take Masaru Ibuka, Sony's co-founder, who often travelled lugging a bulky cassette recorder around to listen to music when he travelled. His workaround led to the development of the Sony Walkman, a portable stereo cassette player.

3. **Look for why people don't buy.** Take the scientists at a major global pharmaceutical company developing a drug for depression that had excellent results but was not selling. They discovered that the side effects of the drug, which could include weight gain and sleep loss, were overriding its benefits. They made modifications resulting in marginally lower performance but far less intrusive side effects. The new drug sold.

> For more examples of observing customers, and workarounds go to:
>
> http://blog.usabilla.com/top-ethnographic-research-videos/

The MVP – try it for real

In his book *The Lean Startup,* Eric Ries introduces the concept of a 'minimum viable product' or MVP. An MVP encompasses the core features of the product required to solicit feedback from customers and feeds directly into the product's development. The crowdfunding platform Kickstarter is an example of how you can test an MVP. It allows you to set up a page for your product, and test different price points or product variations. If people are interested in your product they validate by providing funding. You can test which prices and variations are most appealing to your customer. There is more about Lean Startup methodology in **Step 8** (on **page 100**).

> You can also read more about the Lean Startup at:
>
> http://theleanstartup.com

Some organisations like Procter & Gamble take another approach and involve their customers in product innovation. This is referred to as open innovation and you can learn more in **Skill 5** (on **page 132**).

- What are the things you can do as an innovation ethnographer to observe customers in their natural state?
- What day-to-day activities can you do to get to know your customers better?
- What can you do to encourage others to help learn and share information about customers?

What is insight?

Insight is the capacity to gain an accurate and deep understanding of someone or something.

Gathering data and information is the first stage. Great innovators also consider what the information means. Insight is about asking, *'If this is what we know about the customer, what does that mean for our organisation and what opportunities could it provide us with to meet both our needs and theirs?'*

The skill of a great innovator is not necessarily knowing that a customer does something but *why* they do it. For example, consumers worry about germs in the bathroom and believe they hang out in hard to reach places. *Toilet Duck* responds to this with bleach that can get to hard to reach places. Or clubbers who want a drink to enhance their clubbing experience. *Red Bull* is a mixer drink that gives a massive energy boost so clubbers can keep clubbing all night without getting too drunk.

Ask the question 'If this is what we know about what our customers want, then what could that *mean* for the products and services we develop?'

What does it mean?

Using personas

A tool to help you think about what the information you have gathered means is the persona template. It helps you to paint a picture of a customer and turn the information you have into insight, through asking questions that you would not ask them directly, for example considering what might keep them awake at night. If you know what keeps them awake, you can think about solutions to help them sleep!

Personas are also a good way to help you think from your customer's perspective when you don't know much about your customer. Even if in lieu of having any information, you make some assumptions about your customer, trying to think from their perspective is still a valuable innovation exercise.

Download the persona template on page 8 of the innovation toolkit from www.thebusinessgym.net and complete it for one of your customers. What insights did you come up with?

Case study

Knowing what customers want before they do

In the 1980s, if you wanted to do any type of banking transaction, apart from withdrawing cash at an ATM, you had to show up at your bank and join a queue to be seen by someone behind the counter. If the only time that you could go was in your lunch hour you often spent the whole hour patiently waiting in a queue.

That was until 1 October 1989 when First Direct burst into the banking market. Inspired by insight that younger customers wanted greater control of their finances and the flexibility to carry out transactions at times that suited them, First Direct pioneered the UK's first telephone banking service. Despite the fact that this new 24/7 telephone banking would make it easier and quicker for people to manage their finances on their terms, First Direct was ridiculed. It was initially dismissed by rival banks, which largely failed to understand why any customer would want 24-hour access to their bank account.

The media also made fun of it, *The Independent* apparently dubbing it as 'a service for bored insomniacs'.

Sceptics said it would not work, because they could not understand how anything could replace the face-to-face service that customers received in high street branches.

Looking back now, it's hard to believe that people only had one option of physically going to a bank to make transactions for so long. Today contacting our banks through telephone, the internet and SMS is the 'normal' way of banking. When was the last time you went and queued at the bank to speak to a person about your finances?

First Direct identified a problem that customers had not really been aware of, the problem of the inflexibility of having to physically go to a bank to conduct transactions. Even though it seems really obvious today, back then if you had asked customers what they wanted they wouldn't have known that telephone banking was a solution because they hadn't experienced it and the flexibility it would bring.

Since launching, First Direct has been open every single day. Today First Direct has over 1.25 million customers and is often cited as one of the UK's most successful consumer brands renowned for excellent levels of customer service.

In this step about knowing and understanding your customers, the essential innovation principles to remember are:

- Understanding your customers will help you develop better innovations.
- Focus groups and surveys need to be considered carefully as what people say they do and what they actually do are often different.
- Become an ethnographer – use as many tactics as you can to hang out with, observe and listen to your customers on a day-to-day basis.
- Use personas to help you think more deeply about your customers.
- Turn your information into insight by considering, if this is the information, then what does it *mean*?

If you are reading this book step by step, before you move on to Step 3 make sure you are clear on who your customer is and have thought about them in more detail by filling out the persona template on page 8 of the innovation toolkit at:

www.thebusinessgym.net

Call to action

Go and talk with a customer you are doing the persona for and report back on what you learned about them and what they think about your company or product.

If you could take one idea from this step to practise in your day-to-day work, what would it be?

_____

_____

_____

Step 3

Your market today and predicting the trends of tomorrow

After reading this step you will learn how to:

- Understand the marketplace that your customers operate in
- Discover more information from your competitors according to what they are succeeding and failing at
- Look for trends to help you develop ideas for future innovation opportunities.

'**Your success in life isn't based on your ability to simply change.
It is based on your ability to change faster than your competition,
customers, and business.**'

Mark Sanborn, Leadership speaker

The story so far

In the last step we learned that defining your customer and then
working at understanding what makes them tick gives you the
best chance of developing successful ideas and innovations. You
also started to think and practise turning knowledge into insight.

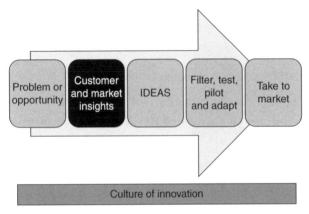

Steps for successful innovation

Why it is important to understand the marketplace

No idea operates in a vacuum: it doesn't matter how big or small your
idea is, its success is dictated by how it operates in a marketplace.
Markets change constantly, at different speeds, but everything
is influenced by things that are beyond your control. For example,
there could be a price increase in the raw material you need for your
product. For a pizza restaurant, a change in the price of tomatoes
could potentially have a big impact on its profit margin. To maintain
margins, the restaurant has choices: put the price up and risk losing
customers, use fewer tomatoes and risk a lower quality product,
do nothing and take the hit and hope the price reduces, or diversify
to a tomato-less pizza product (or something more appealing!). Or
perhaps the restaurant saw it coming and bought big supplies of
tomatoes in advance of the price hike to make into sauce and freeze.

Whatever your core business, your marketplace is constantly changing. If you do nothing, or spend too long deciding what to do, your competitors, suppliers and customers will all be responding to the change, and failure to respond could put you out of business. Just like Kodak.

 For more about failure and Kodak go to:
www.thebusinessgym.net

How to get information on your current marketplace

There is lots of information available, both free and paid for, that you can use to paint a picture of your current market, including the following.

Published research information

Marketing reports, for example, can help you understand how big your overall market is, whether it is growing or declining, what the trends are and what competitive products are available.

Past trends

Data research, market research reports and trade association press could help you look at past trends for your products and the marketplace to form a picture of the reasons for the current market situations.

Demographic information

Demographic information, for example about your target audience, can be obtained via the Office for National Statistics (**www.statistics.gov.uk**). This includes information on the social, economic, business and regional areas.

Regional information

For local area/business information look at regional directories and publications or your local Chamber of Commerce.

Market and consumer trends

Read your trade magazines, attend exhibitions and trade fairs. Follow thought leaders in your field on blogs and social media.

Suppliers and distributors

Build relationships, keep in touch: you will gain insight on current trends from working with others in the marketplace.

Your competitors

Smart innovators keep up to date with their competitors.

- Who are your direct competitors? List at least five.
- Who are the indirect competitors? For example, the pizza restaurant is competing directly with other pizza restaurants, but also the fried chicken shop and the burger joint. Who are yours?
- What does their business look like: is it growing, declining or steady?
- How does their product or service differ from yours?
- What are their strengths and weaknesses?
- What can you learn from how they operate, their marketing messages, how they position themselves?

If you answered 'don't know' to any of the above then it's time to find out!

Mystery shop

Become a customer. You can learn so much about your competitors from picking apart their products and offerings and applying the good ideas to your own, as well as learning what not to do from poor product and service experiences.

You are not a lone crusader in the quest for market and competitor information. Recruit friends and colleagues to mystery shop and then tell you about their experiences. You will build a bigger picture more quickly and will benefit from the different perspectives of a team of people gathering insight.

Public information

Keep up to date with company reports and accounts, catalogues and websites. What are they offering their customers?

How to predict future trends

Understanding your current environment is a good starting point. However, that is only information about now, or things that have already happened. A more crucial innovation skill, especially if you are developing products and services that will not be in the marketplace until sometime in the future, is being able to understand what is likely to be happening when your products are live. I know that being able to predict the future might sound like a tall order, but anticipating future trends is not as far-fetched as it might initially sound.

 Check out this TED Talk from Alison Sander on Megatrends – the art and science of trend tracking:

www.ted.com/watch/ted-institute/ted-bcg/alison-sander-megatrends-the-art-and-science-of-trend-tracking

Here are some practical ways that you can start to build your trend spotter superpowers.

Observe more

Get into the habit of spotting what is happening by keeping up with social, economic and environmental trends. All things are connected so what is happening today will inform future trends. Read newspapers and magazines. Read popular blogs. Watch TV, not just the news but popular shows.

Trend reports

Buy (and read!) trend reports for your sector or industry.

Look outside your sector

What are the trends that haven't affected your business yet? What are the regulatory, economic, legal, technological and social issues that are likely to affect your idea in the future? For example, if consumers are purchasing more by mobile, if this trend continues to grow, what impact would this have on your business? If you knew that mobile was going to be the only method of payment in the future, what would you need to do to be ready one year from now? If house prices or interest rates are going up what does that mean for your organisation? How will the rise in interest rates affect your customers or your suppliers?

Big data

This is defined as extremely large data sets, for example from phones, credit cards, televisions and computers, that may be analysed to reveal patterns, trends and associations, especially relating to human behaviour and interactions. This opens up some incredible insights:

- Google has analysed search terms clustered by region in the US to predict flu outbreaks faster than hospital administration records.[3]
- Target in the US infamously used an algorithm that tracked purchases of items such as unscented lotions to detect when women were pregnant and offered discounts to them.[4]
- Propeller Health (was Asthmapolis) in the US conducted tests with asthmatic school children. A GPS sensor in their inhalers recorded their location whenever they used them. The aggregated data showed that proximity to a refinery aggravated the children's asthma. A simple solution of taking a different route significantly reduced the incidences of asthma.[5]

Online option for big data blog

Free data on new innovation is available so set up relevant news feeds to the abundance of free online data, blogs and reports that is out there. There are some sites that aggregate new innovation ideas and top trending stories all in one place, for example:

- Springwise **www.springwise.com**
- PSFK **www.psfk.com**
- Alltop **http://alltop.com**
- Mashable **http://mashable.com**

[3]Google.org Flu Trends, 2011. *Google.org*. Available at: <https://www.google.org/flutrends/about/how.html>

[4]Duhigg, C. (2012) How companies learn your secrets. The New York Times Magazine. Available at: <http://www.nytimes.com/2012/02/19/magazine/shopping-habits.html?pagewanted=1&_r=1&hp>

[5]Comstock, J. (2013) Asthmapolis, now Propeller, moves beyond asthma. Available at: <http://mobihealthnews.com/25255/asthmapolis-now-propeller-moves-beyond-asthma/> Klein, S. (2011) Q&A – Asthmapolis: Improving asthma control with mobile technology. Quality Matters. Available at: <http://www.commonwealthfund.org/publications/newsletters/quality-matters/2011/october-november-2011/q-a>

- BuzzFeed **www.buzzfeed.com**
- trendwatching.com **http://trendwatching.com/tips-tools**
- Trend Hunter **www.trendhunter.com**

Of course, the problem with the above is that everyone else looking to build their trend spotter superpowers is looking there too. So you have to trend spot the emerging trend spotting places to keep ahead of the other trend spotters!

If you understand that, then also consider getting ahead by looking at:

- **Who is making money?** Look at the fastest growing companies to see where their profits are coming from. What does that mean for your ideas?
- **Teenagers:** they know about trends. Also ask students where they want to work after graduation for an indication of the industries and areas that these groups are aspiring to.
- **Startups:** look at the commonalities between the latest startups, what are the themes that connect their ideas?
- **Frequency:** if something gets written or talked about across different media at least three times, then that is an indicator that it could become a trend. What topics are you seeing cropping up again and again in the media?
- **Different industries:** what is trending in one industry or category that can be exported to transform yours? For example, the trend for low carb diets saw Pret A Manger developing low carb salads and sandwich offerings. How could this translate into the frozen product marketplace or restaurant menu choices?
- **What culture shifts are happening?** Where are people spending their time doing something that they don't have to do? Where are they fiddling with tools, coining new lingo, swapping new techniques? That's where culture is created. For example, CRUK used the increased popularity of smartphone gaming to develop a game to identify cancer cells called Cell Slider. At the time of writing the game had been downloaded by over 500,000 people, who together are helping CRUK achieve their goal of beating cancer faster.

Automate your search

Technology can help you automate your search for trends, for example:

- YouTube trends dashboard **www.youtube.com/trends dashboard** will tell you the popularity of video content.
- Google Alerts can send you daily information based on your search terms, so for example, you could search for when your company name, or that of your competitors, is mentioned, or for search terms relating to your product or idea.

 For more on becoming a trend guru go to:

http://trendwatching.com/tips-tools

In the same way as you did with customer insight, when thinking about the marketplace today and future trends, you need to ask yourself, 'If this is the information, if this is what I know – then what does it *mean* for me, for my business and my ideas?'

 Practice this skill and try the 'turning insight into action' exercise on page 13 of the innovation toolkit. You can download this from:

www.thebusinessgym.net

And finally, understanding your customers, marketplace and competitors is not just an exercise to do at the start of the innovation process, it is critical to continue to increase your understanding as you develop existing products and look for opportunities and inspiration.

 Set some SMART objectives

What things are you going to do to understand your current market? Make them specific, measurable, achievable, realistic and timely (i.e. SMART).

For example, can you spend 20 minutes a day reading about your sector marketplace?

What things are you going to do to understand competitors? For example, mystery shop one competitor a week and report back to the team on the experience and consider what you can implement in your team.

What activities are you going to do to become a trend spotting superhero? For example, read about the latest innovations in your sector for an hour each week.

In this step about your market today and predicting the trends of tomorrow, the essential innovation principles to remember are:

- In addition to understanding your customers, understanding the marketplace they operate in will help you spot opportunities.
- Dedicate time to understanding your current marketplace and your competition.
- Observe more from outside your sector, including social, environmental and economic factors, because you don't operate in a vacuum – everything is connected.
- Seek future trends to help you spot opportunities for ideas and innovation.

Call to action

If you are reading this book step by step, before you move on to **Step 4**, complete the actions in this step and do some research to better understand your market, competitors and trends.

If you could take one idea from this step to practise in your day-to-day work, what would it be?

_____

_____

_____

Step 4

Build your creative capacity

After reading this step you will learn how to:

- Increase your personal capacity for having ideas
- Break patterns in your behaviour to help broaden your thinking skills through expanding your experiences
- Collect and record ideas and practise connecting new ideas.

'Creativity is the ability to see relationships where none exist.'

Thomas Disch, Sci-fi writer and poet

The story so far

In the last step you learned to get really smart at understanding not just the marketplace of today but how your markets could look in the future. You have tactics to find this information and make seeking it out a habit. It's not just a case of gathering information though, it's about challenging yourself to practise the art of thinking, 'If this is what I know then what does it *mean*?'

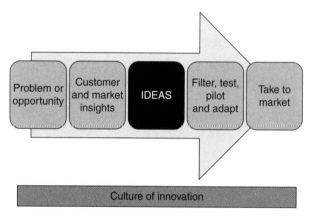

Steps for successful innovation

Where do ideas come from?

There is a myth that ideas are created in a darkened room by a lone genius, often referred to as the light bulb moment. While some of us might do our best thinking alone, innovation rarely happens in a vacuum.

Steven Johnson, in his book *Where Good Ideas Come From,* describes having ideas as more of a process of slow hunches than a eureka moment and that the best ideas come from building on and connecting the ideas and inventions of others. This means that being able to make connections is a critical innovation skill.

 Watch Steven Johnson talk more about where ideas come from on TED:

https://www.ted.com/playlists/20/where_do_ideas_come_from

Steven Johnson is not the only expert to identify that ideas are not new in themselves but a combination of ideas that have gone before fused together in new ways. In the 1940s James Webb Young published a book called *A Technique for Producing Ideas* which begins with the premise that an idea is nothing more or less than a new combination of old elements. And that the key to an effective idea process is an individual's ability to search for relationships between elements that turn separate unconnected bits of knowledge into something greater. You can read more about innovation by imitation in **Skill 8** on **page 144.**

Steve Jobs in his 2005 commencement speech at Stanford, refers to the same principle as 'joining the dots'. He tells the story of when he dropped out of college and how it gave him the opportunity to drop in on classes that looked interesting. He decided to take a calligraphy class that had no practical application for him at the time, but looking back 10 years later this knowledge was pivotal in creating the fonts and typefaces for Apple Macintosh products.

Jobs said, 'You can't connect the dots looking forward; you can only connect them looking backwards. So you have to trust that the dots will somehow connect in your future.'

 See Jobs' full speech at:

www.youtube.com/watch?v=D1R-jKKp3NA

Experience more

If you have different experiences, you have more material to make connections with. So you have to increase your experience quota. Simple.

Some organisations actively encourage their employees to have new ideas. The most famous of these is Google and its 'innovation time off' policy, which requires engineers to spend 20 per cent of their time on their own projects guided by their own passions and interests.

How to have more experiences

Find things that you are curious or passionate about in the same way that Steve Jobs was about his calligraphy classes or

Google engineers are about their own projects. Here are some suggestions:

- Travel to a place you have never been to before.
- Learn a new skill (e.g. a new language, calligraphy).
- Do something that scares you.
- Do an activity, for example, singing or dancing.
- Take improvisation classes.
- Learn a traditional skill, like cooking, sewing or gardening.
- Do something that you have always wanted to do but keep putting off.
- Ask children for their ideas of a fun thing to try – then do it.
- Volunteer for something.

You can make expanding your experience as simple or as complex as you like. The point is that in order to develop your innovation skills you need a breadth of experiences to draw on. Think of it as your resource bank and to keep a healthy balance you need to keep adding to it.

Breaking out of everyday patterns

We are all creative and capable of having ideas, but how our creativity manifests itself is different for every one of us. However, as we grow older we learn in education and then in the workplace that we get rewarded for getting things right, following instructions and getting the job done – and not for inquisitive enquiry, experimenting or ideas, and certainly not for getting things wrong. Ken Robinson, author, speaker and international advisor on education in the arts to government in the UK, is critical of the education system in the UK for its role in inhibiting creative thinking. One of the results of this is that we tend to stick to what we know, to safe situations and habits that we repeat over and over again. While this in some ways can be helpful, for example we know a system works and we continue to use it in that way, the risk is, that if we only do more of the same, or we don't adapt quickly enough, we follow in the footsteps of Kodak, Blockbuster and HMV. They no longer exist.

Listen to Ken Robinson on how schools kill creativity on TED:

www.ted.com/talks/ken_robinson_says_schools_kill_creativity?language=en

Dr Simone Ritter from Radboud University conducted research as to whether new and unexpected experiences boost your creativity. She ran a series of experiments in which volunteers experienced a virtual world that did not follow the normal rules, for example things got smaller as they approached them and objects defied gravity. She also set volunteers everyday tasks where they followed a script that forced them to complete the task in a way that was different from 'normal', for example making a sandwich.

Volunteers then took a creative thinking test. Their creativity scores increased by 15 per cent. Ritter describes a concept of 'functional fixitness', which is when our thinking gets stuck in a rut.[6] We overcome this through building new associations between concepts. Changing your routine forces you to abandon well-travelled neural pathways which forces new connections between brain cells which in turn leads to new and original ideas.

So as well as expanding your experience portfolio you need to break out of those routines that you complete mindlessly day after day without noticing what is around you. Here are some ways you can do this:

- Take a different route to work and notice what is around you.
- Read a different newspaper and see the world from a different perspective.
- Listen to a different radio station.
- Eat or drink in a different restaurant or bar.
- Go to a different place for lunch and try something new.
- Change TV channel – or turn the TV off completely and do something different instead.
- Sit at a different desk in the office.

[6]*Horizon, The creative brain: how insight works,* series 49, episode 8. [TV programme] BBC2, 14 March 2013.

- Hold your meetings in a different location to normal, and at different times, for example 9.25am. (Who made the rules that meetings start on the hour or half hour and come in 30 minute chunks?)
- Have lunch with someone from a different team.
- Watch a film that is completely different to what you would usually watch.

Order and catalogue your thoughts

In *A Technique for Producing Ideas,* James Webb Young highlights the importance of ordering and cataloguing your thoughts. He talks about Sherlock Holmes who spent hours indexing and cross-indexing his thoughts in scrapbooks. Young was writing in the 1940s and today there are many more ways of recording and ordering your thoughts. You too could keep a scrapbook like Sherlock Holmes, but the most important point is to find a way that makes it easy for you. This could be a scrapbook, a notebook, taking photos. Alternatively, you might prefer to use online tools to gather your ideas and share them in one place, for example:

- Pinterest – a free online notice board where you can 'pin' images and web content including video and invite others to contribute.
- Your own blog – there are free platforms, for example WordPress, where you can post your thoughts and ideas.
- SlideShare– a free site where you can upload and share your presentations.

There is no right or wrong way; success is finding a system that works for *you.*

And relax . . .

Did you ever have your best idea when you were at work at your desk? If you answer yes to this, you are in a special minority of exquisite thinkers. Most of us have our best ideas when we are relaxed (which for most of us is not when we are at our desks). So a genuine technique for innovation is to go and relax and put the whole problem out of your mind.

Go and do something else, anything else that relaxes you: have a nap, go for a walk, read a novel, go to the movies, go to the gym or phone a friend. This is a definite and necessary stage that allows your subconscious mind to process your thoughts. The expression 'sleep on it' has truth to it.

Mindfulness and innovation

Mindfulness, meaning paying attention to, and living in the moment, has also become a no substance corporate buzzword. Given the pressure in today's world to be constantly connected and partially focused on multiple tasks, constantly interrupted and bombarded with information, it's no wonder that mindfulness is gaining popularity.

Rooted in Buddhism and other Eastern philosophies mindfulness is being reviewed as more than just a way to cope with the anxiety associated with constant connectivity and multitasking business demands. Instead, it's being advocated by corporations including Google, Walt Disney and General Mills as having a key role in driving creativity and innovation.

Research has shown that people who meditate have greater cognitive rigidity and flexibility to solve problems in more creative ways than those who don't. A *Wired* report on Silicon Valley's meditation habit cites 'meditation here isn't an opportunity to reflect upon the impermanence of existence but a tool to better oneself and improve productivity'.[7]

Three ways to be more mindful

- Practise just sitting for five minutes without being distracted by anything else.
- Next time you are stuck on a problem take some time out to be quiet and allow your stress to subside by focusing on your breath for a few minutes.
- Regular meditation practice will help you learn skills to train your mind and calm your emotions, allowing your creativity to flow.

[7]Shactman, N. (2013) In Silicon Valley, meditation is no fad. It could make your career. *Wired* [online]. Available at: <http://www.wired.com/2013/06/meditation-mindfulness-silicon-valley/201>

Connecting ideas

When you have ordered and catalogued your thoughts and experiences, then start to look for relationships that could form new ideas.

There are many examples where relationships between two different ideas have resulted in a new innovation:

- In 1440 Johannes Gutenberg, a goldsmith and a businessman, combined the wine press with a coin punch and invented the printing press. This method of printing was revolutionary for the production of books and also the rapid sharing of knowledge and development in the sciences, arts and religion.
- In 1970 Bernard Sadow was coming home from holiday and noticed a worker at the airport pushing a machine on a wheeled pallet. He had the idea to combine wheels with the heavy suitcase he had been dragging around to invent the wheeled suitcase.
- A bit more recently, in 2006, Trunki combined ride on toys and a suitcase to invent ride on hand luggage for children, a combination that gives children the responsibility for their possessions as well as something to play with when going on holiday.

Write down your random thoughts and possible connections and keep building ideas. Get into the habit of doing it regularly. The more you practise, the easier it will become and the better you will get. Don't edit or filter, just write everything that comes to your mind.

 Mix and mismatch

This exercise is designed to help you practise and increase your confidence in making connections.

Materials: two packs of *Post-it Notes*, a pen and a wall to stick them on.

- Decide on the topic that you are going to connect ideas about, for example a Christmas product.
- Decide on the audience, for example, pets.

- Spend two minutes writing down everything that you think of when you say the word 'Christmas'. Write each word on a different *Post-it Note*. Don't filter; write down everything that comes into your head. (Even if the words are nothing to do with Christmas, even if you repeat words, just keep going for two minutes.) After two minutes you should have a pile of *Post-it Notes.*
- Now spend two minutes writing everything that you think of when you think of pets. Same rules apply as before, write everything and don't filter.
- Now you should have two piles of *Post-it Notes* with words on.
- Stick them on the wall – Christmas on the left and pets on the right.
- Now mix them up to make as many combinations as you can. Don't try to put words together that feel like they fit such as dog + sled. Randomly put the words together.
- You should now have lots of pairs of *Post-it Notes* that mix Christmas-inspired words with pet-inspired words.
- Now quickly go through the word pairs and force product ideas from the word combinations. For example, for cat and reindeer you might come up with reindeer outfits for cats, reindeer antlers for cats, reindeer cat toys, Rudolf noses for cats, red cat noses for humans, reindeer harness for cats, reindeer food for cats. Or you might come up with something better!

Remember this exercise is not about coming up with sensible products. It is about practising making connections. I don't care if you come up with 50 ridiculous ideas. In fact that is exactly the point. To allow yourself to connect random ideas and to be bold enough to say them out loud!

You can do this on your own or in groups. You can use any combination of topics for this exercise, the more unrelated the better to force ideas about anything at all. You could even turn this game into a competition: who can come up with the most ridiculous, rude or random idea? The key purpose of this exercise is to get your brain working to connect unrelated topics. It's the process that is important.

 ## SMART objectives

Think about the sections in this step and answer the following questions with SMART objectives:

- What are the things that you are curious about? What are you going to do to expand your experience in those areas?
- How can you break some of your day-to-day routines that you do without even thinking?
- How can you catalogue your thoughts?
- Where do you have your best ideas?
- How can you make being mindful/relaxed part of your everyday habits?

In this step about building your creative capacity, the essential innovation principles to remember are:

- Expand your experiences by learning and doing new things.
- Get out of a rut and improve your creativity by breaking patterns in your daily routine.
- Find a way that makes it easy for you to order and catalogue your thoughts.
- Look after yourself, consider your wellbeing and take time to switch off so your subconscious brain can work on ideas.
- Make connections between unrelated topics.

Call to action

If you are reading this book step by step, before you move on to **Step 5** make sure you have done the mix and mismatch exercise to practise connecting new ideas and start to make breaking daily routines a habit.

If you could take one idea from this step to practise in your day-to-day work, what would it be?

_____

_____

_____

Step 5

Creative superstardom and lots of ideas

After reading this step you will learn how to:

- Discover what can inhibit your creativity
- Test out some techniques to help you and your colleagues generate lots of ideas
- Come up with multiple solutions for problems and not stop at your first idea.

'We cannot solve our problems by using the same kind of thinking we used when we created them.'

Albert Einstein, Nobel Prize in Physics

The story so far

In the last step you were told to get out more! Getting out more helps to expand your experiences and gives you more material to combine into new ideas. If you have been out and tried something new since you read the last step you are now ready for **Step 5**.

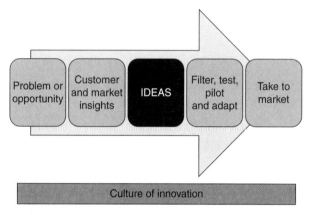

Steps for successful innovation

What pets do these people own?

I suspect that you made some guesses: the man in the striped hat keeps tropical fish, the couple has a dog, perhaps a small terrier, and the young woman has a cat, or several cats.

We all make stereotypes or assumptions based on what we already know, or things that have been proven to us from our experiences to be true in the past. This is how our brains work. It makes us efficient. It means we don't have to learn things from scratch every time we do something. However, when we are trying to come up with ideas it can inhibit our creativity because we make assumptions about what is or is not possible. If anyone has ever helpfully killed your idea by saying something like, 'We tried that before, and it didn't work' then you will have felt the negative and inhibiting power of assumptions.

One way to practise challenging your assumptions, exercise your innovation muscles and engage all the parts of your brain is through solving lateral thinking puzzles, which requires an indirect or creative approach.

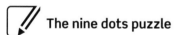 **The nine dots puzzle**

Draw four straight lines which will cross through all nine dots (without lifting your pencil from the page).

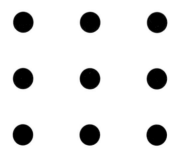

The answer is on **page 216** at the end of the book.

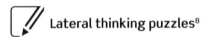

Lateral thinking puzzles[8]

Challenge your own assumptions and ask 'why?' more. What solutions can you come up with for the scenarios below? For any problem there can be many solutions. Write down as many as you can. It's not just about seeking the *right* answer it's about exercising your brain to come up with as many solutions as possible. These are all real problems and the solutions that were chosen are on **page 215.**

Shoe shop shuffle

In a small town there are four shoe shops of about the same size and each carries a similar line of shoes. Yet one shop loses three times as many shoes to theft as each of the other shops. Why was this and how did they fix the problem?

The school inspection

A school teacher knew that the school inspector would visit the next day. The inspector would ask questions such as spellings or mental arithmetic of the class, and the teacher would choose a pupil to answer. The teacher wanted to give the best impression of the school. What instructions did she give the children in order to present the best impression and maximise the chances that the right answer would be given to each question?

Wrong number

The marketing department of a major bank prepared a direct mail campaign to launch a new product. They printed over 2 million brochures but were horrified to find a mistake in the brochure – it had a wrong digit in the telephone number. Callers would get a dead line instead of the call centre. What should they do first – fire the marketing manager or reprint the brochures?

Price tag

Many shops have prices set at just under a round figure, such as £9.99 instead of £10 or £99.95 instead of £100. It is often assumed that this is done to make the prices appear lower to the consumer. But this is not the reason the practice started. What was the original reason for this pricing method?

Answers are on **page 215.**

[8]Based on puzzles which appeared in Sloane, P. , (2006) *The Leader's Guide to Lateral Thinking Skills*, Kogan Page

You can continue to practise lateral thinking puzzles:
www.kent.ac.uk/careers/sk/lateral.htm

Breaking patterns to help generate ideas

You have already learned some tactics in **Step 4** about breaking patterns in everyday life. When we are generating ideas it helps to use techniques to break some of our assumptions and ingrained patterns of thinking. What follows are some techniques that you can use. Give them all a go, some resonate more for some people than others. I get so many ideas from technique 1: Ask 'What if?', but we are all different, so you have to find the technique that best triggers *your* creativity.

First let's set some rules. Idea generation is about generating lots and lots of ideas. This is the part of the innovation process where the expression 'no idea is a bad idea' becomes your mantra. The objective is to get as many ideas recorded as possible, no matter how ridiculous they sound.

It is important in the first instance to get all the ideas out there. The weaker or unworkable ideas get filtered out later in the process. We discuss this in **Step 6**.

When you are generating ideas about your innovation topic, remember **Step 1** and frame it as a question: 'How might we . . . ?' Consider the work you did on customers and the marketplace. You are looking for ideas to solve your problem based on insights about your customer, so a question could be something like: 'How might we provide the best customer service for our online customers?'

 Technique 1: Ask 'What if?'

This technique is about throwing away the rules and addressing your assumptions head on about how things are usually done.

Take the rules of what you are innovating around. For example, a customer newsletter, what are the rules? Is it always printed? Does it always follow the same format? Is it sent on the same day each month? Is there always a boring paragraph on progress this month from the senior team?

Write down all the rules that you can think of.

Now mess with these rules. Take one rule, e.g. what if it wasn't printed then what would it be, an email, an audio, a face-to-face meeting, carried by a pigeon? (Remember all ideas get written down at this point!)

Come up with as many ideas as you can. Write them all down. Do it quickly. Don't over analyse.

 Technique 2: Make it fun

Making it fun is a similar principle to 'What if?' because it breaks the rules by asking the question, what could we do to make this fun?

Consider the problem that you are working on. Think about what you know about your customers and the marketplace.

Come up with as many FUN ideas as you can to solve your problem. Write them all down.

Do it quickly. Don't over analyse.

Case study

How to stop people jaywalking

The problem that the team at Smart wanted to solve was to stop people jaywalking at pedestrian crossings. They wanted to get people to wait for the green man before stepping out into the road. They focused on making it fun. They came up with the Dancing Traffic Light, an experiential marketing concept

Source: Berkowitz, J. (2014) Jaywalking is unsafe, so this interactive campaign offers dance breaks instead. *Fast Company* [online] Available at: <http://www.fastcocreate.com/3035929/gif-of-the-day/jaywalking-is-unsafe-so-this-interactive-campaign-offers-dance-breaks-instead>

providing a fun and safe way to keep people from venturing too early into the street. They started by placing a dance room on a square in Lisbon, Portugal and invited random pedestrians to go into the box and dance. Their movements were then displayed on a few red traffic lights in real time. This resulted in 81 per cent more people stopping and waiting at those red lights.

 You can see more examples of fun innovation at:
www.thefuntheory.com

 Technique 3: Where else in the world?

Think about where else in the world your problem has been solved. It could be in a different context or a different sector. Think about how people solved the problem and what elements of it you can adapt for your context. Just as innovation is a combination of old ideas put together in new ways, innovation can also be solutions used somewhere else and applied to your context.

List all the different worlds that have solved your problem. For example, if your customers are leaving because of poor service, who else has turned a business around by keeping customers: First Direct, Zappos, your local takeaway? List as many as you can. Research what they did. Better still see if you can talk to them. You may be surprised at how much people are willing to share.

Especially if you are thoughtful and flattering about your approach: for example, something like 'I've admired how you solved this difficult problem, I am working on something similar in my sector, I wondered if you would be able to share your expert knowledge?'

Case study

ColaLife

One child in every eight dies before their fifth birthday from simple preventable causes, such as dehydration from diarrhoea. In these same places where clean water and medicine are hard to find, people can still buy Coke.

In 1988, Simon Berry was an aid worker in Africa who asked if Coca-Cola's local distribution networks could be used to deliver life-saving medicines to hard-to-reach places.

Twenty years later, Simon and his partner Jane launched ColaLife, an independent not-for-profit organisation to work with Coca-Cola to do just that.

Simon's first idea was to remove a Coke bottle from one in 10 crates and put a tube filled with medicine in the space. With the help of the online following that Simon grew through regular blogs, Facebook and Twitter updates, the idea developed into a wedge shaped 'AidPod' that slotted into the unused space between the bottles. The 'AidPod' was further developed, with help from rural mothers, as an 'anti-diarrhoea kit' containing small sachets of oral rehydration salts, zinc tablets and soap for hand washing. The kit container also acts as a measuring device for the water needed to mix the salts, a mixing and a storage device.

The kits are promoted through rural health centres by community health workers. Retailers travel to the nearest district town to buy the kits the same way they do for other fast moving consumer goods such as Coca-Cola, cooking oil, salt and sugar.

Simon Berry said: 'We wanted our diarrhoea treatment kits to be as ubiquitous as Coca-Cola in remote village kiosks so we use existing private sector distribution networks to achieve this goal. The secret is that everyone in the value chain – manufacturer, distributor, wholesaler and retailer – makes a profit. That way, it's a fully sustainable supply network and parents get the medicines they need for their children, closer to their home and at prices most can afford.'

For more information go to: **www.colalife.org**

Technique 4: Someone else's idea

These techniques have all been about changing your mindset, so what better way to do that than to get into someone else's mind. First think of a person or character. It could be someone you know, a character in a film, a historical figure, your granny. The principle is that you are looking for inspiration from someone who has a different perspective from you. The more different they are from you, the more it challenges you to break your 'normal' patterns of thinking. My particular favourites are Homer Simpson, Margaret Thatcher and Kermit the Frog.

Quickly write down all their characteristics; include anything and everything that comes into your head. Don't over analyse and worry about whether Homer eats more donuts than pizza. The point is that you are not thinking from your perspective. Think about what is important to them: what do they have for breakfast, what keeps them awake at night, what do they enjoy doing on a Friday night, what books are they reading, what films do they watch?

Then consider the problem you are generating ideas about. What would this person do?

Write them all down.

Do it quickly. Don't over analyse.

You can use these techniques on your own or they can work well in a group if you are facilitating an ideas session. See **Step 6** for how to run an ideas session.

Here are 13 more unusual idea generation techniques from the Huffington Post:

www.huffingtonpost.com/young-entrepreneur-council/13-unusual-brainstorming_b_3880619.html

In this step about creative superstardom and lots of ideas, the essential innovation principles to remember are:

- Use idea generation techniques to help you to generate greater volumes and variety of ideas.
- Write down all your ideas regardless of how strange they may sound – don't over analyse.

- Check yourself – observe when you make an assumption about something.
- Enjoy the process – have fun.

Call to action

If you are reading this book step by step, before you move on to **Step 6** practise framing your topic as a question: 'How might we . . . ?' then use idea generation techniques and write down all your ideas.

If you could take one idea from this step to practise in your day-to-day work, what would it be?

_____

_____

_____

Step 6

Don't expect anyone else to like your idea

After reading this step you will learn how to:

- Facilitate an excellent ideas workshop with confidence
- Influence others and gain support for your ideas
- Identify win-win situations.

'Don't worry about people stealing an idea. If it's original, you will have to ram it down their throats.'

Howard H. Aiken, computing pioneer

The story so far

In the last step you revisited how to frame your innovation as a question that begins, 'How might we ... ?' as well as considering what you know about your customer. Then with the help of some different techniques you were able to unleash all the creative ideas you could on the matter.

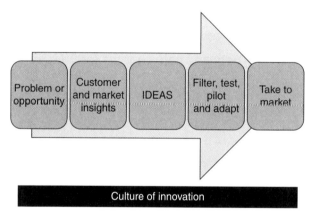

Steps for successful innovation

It is not the shortage of ideas that is the biggest problem for both individuals and organisations when it comes to innovation. Making the ideas happen is much harder. Innovation is all about people. You can have the best processes in place but if you don't have people aligned, passionate about why your innovation matters, your innovation will fail. Involving others is likely to take more time and effort initially and can be frustrating. You also have to become resilient as you overcome objections and try different tactics to win people over. However, it is worth the effort because involving people from the beginning will ultimately increase the chances of your idea happening.

How to involve others with your innovation - facilitate an ideas session

You may have experience of attending or facilitating an ideas session or brainstorm. They are one way to generate and build on ideas, but they also serve another purpose: building relationships and getting buy-in from people you need on board to help make your idea happen, for example funders, partners, suppliers, colleagues and managers. Here are some tactics to help you get the best from people in your next ideas session.

Focus

Inform the participants of why they have been invited and what is in it for them as well as why the innovation problem they are giving up their time to work on really matters. Frame your problem as a question that is broad enough for people to have room to be creative, but defined enough that you will get ideas that are relevant. For example, don't ask people 'How might we sell more products?' Consider something more specific like 'How might we sell more products to working mums online?'

If you have insight about your customer then pick one or two key insights and ask the group to consider that as part of the process.

Independent facilitator

Get a facilitator who can be impartial and is responsible for keeping to topic, who gets the best from everyone in the room and ensures the session runs to time. A good facilitator will ensure that everyone in the room gets heard, including the more reserved people, who perhaps don't feel comfortable speaking up in a group. Facilitators will also use a range of techniques to provoke creative thinking.

Mix of people

The more diverse the group of people, the more likely you are to get a range of different perspectives on your topic. Consider also the people you will need on board when the ideas are developed, for example finance, IT, sales and marketing. Involving them from the beginning will help you further down the line.

Explain how the session will run

A creative session is always in two parts:

- **Part 1 – diverge.** This is about getting lots and lots of ideas. Nothing should be filtered here, anything goes.
- **Part 2 – converge.** This is where you select the ideas that have the most potential to take away and work up in more detail.

Make sure people know what is expected of them – are they diverging or converging? If your session is creative, it is divergent, and its purpose is to generate lots of ideas. Before you start, agree a few ground rules:

- Listen and build on ideas using 'yes and' instead of 'no but'.
- No hierarchy – everyone is equal.
- Quantity – it's about lots of ideas no matter how crazy they initially sound.
- No idea killers – for example, 'We've done it before, it didn't work'; 'we don't have a budget'; we won't get it signed off'. None of these phrases that destroy creativity is allowed at this stage.
- Have fun – creating a playful atmosphere helps creativity flow.

Physical environment

Find somewhere away from the office where people feel relaxed, for example an external meeting space or even a local café or the park. Think about the context of the session: for example if you are considering ideas for a new restaurant menu, you could hold the session in a restaurant. If you can't leave the building do what you can to make the environment you have as relaxed as possible with food, music, any props that relate to the subject matter.

Timing

Consider the time of day that will be best for people. Morning sessions tend to be more productive than in the afternoon when everyone is lethargic as they digest their lunch. Make the sessions as long as they need to be. There is no rulebook that says they have to be a set time; 10 minutes, an hour, five hours. Use common sense and make it as long or as short as it needs to be.

Use creative techniques

Use different techniques to warm people up and also to break patterns. This way you will have more chances to appeal to more people's creative preferences. Fight the temptation to stop at your first good idea. The first good idea may be OK, but there is often something better than OK if you give it more time and effort.

Look after your participants

The people who attend your ideas session are your closest allies, so give them a great experience. Thank them for showing up; give them an opportunity to input after the session. Let people know what happens next. Use the session as an excuse to follow up with people one to one to keep them engaged after the session.

Plan

Allow enough time to plan, think about who you invite, find a venue and ensure you have the capacity to follow up. Provide refreshments. Think about how you can make it an inspiring experience that makes people want to come back and work with you.

Manage expectations

View your creative sessions as part of the process. It can be helpful to spend the last few minutes of an ideas workshop asking people to pick their strongest ideas.

Give them guidance so you don't just get personal favourites or the funny/quirky option only because it's appealing to people's sense of humour. Instead ensure that they make their choices based on:

- Does the idea address the purpose?
- Does it respond to some insight?
- Can it be done?

It might not provide one clear solution, but it will help you to give the group a sense of the ideas with the most support as well as signal to the group that they are an important and listened to part of the innovation process.

Workshop planning template
- ☐ Purpose of workshop

☐ Date	☐ Venue
☐ Time	☐ Key contact (external venue)
☐ Facilitator(s)	☐ Invites
☐ Participants	☐ Homework
☐ Refreshments/catering	

Materials check-list

☐ Flip chart	☐ Screen
☐ Post-it notes	☐ Flip chart pens
☐ Blu-Tak/masking tape	☐ Coloured pens
☐ Laptop	☐ Connectors/adapters
☐ Camera/audio	☐ WiFi
☐ Data projector	☐ Directions
☐ Speakers	☐ Name badges

Agenda check-list

☐ Timings	☐ Breaks planned
☐ Warm-up	☐ Space for discussion
☐ Creative thinking technique	☐ Filtering ideas
☐ Rules	☐ Close and next steps

What does success look like?
For example, lots of ideas, or three great ideas to progress, or buy in from the finance team.

Post-workshop

☐ Evaluation	☐ What worked
☐ Send outputs	☐ What didn't work
☐ Send thank yous	☐ Keep updated with progress

Practise and run your own workshop by downloading the workshop planning template on page 23 of the innovation toolkit at:

www.thebusinessgym.net

Ideas without influence lead to innovations without results

In 1984, Dr Robert B. Cialdini published his book *Influence*.[9] It explains the psychology of why people say yes and helps you apply the theory through six simple universal principles. To be a successful innovator you need to get people to say yes to your idea. Use the following universal principles to increase your chances of people saying yes to you:

- **Reciprocity:** if you give then you receive. People are more likely to say yes to those that they owe. Help others, listen and build on their ideas before asking for help with your own.

[9]Cialdini, R. B., 2007. *Influence*. HarperBusiness.

- **Scarcity:** people want more of what there is less of. It's not enough just to tell people the benefits of your innovation idea, explain why this is a unique opportunity and what they stand to lose if they don't get involved.
- **Authority:** people follow the lead of credible experts. Signal to others what makes you a credible knowledgeable authority, for example qualifications or years of experience, before you influence. Or if you are not that person yet, find a credible person to work with you.
- **Commitment and consistency:** people are more likely to commit to something if they have already made a smaller commitment. Start to influence by asking first for small commitments, for example this could be taking part in an ideas workshop.
- **Liking:** people prefer to say yes to people they like. We also like people who are similar to us. Spend time exchanging personal information and building rapport before you attempt to influence.
- **Consensus:** people will look to the actions and behaviours of others before determining their own behaviour (especially if the others are people 'like them'). Show people how 'other people like them' have benefited from saying yes.

 You can see more about Cialdini's principles here:

www.youtube.com/watch?v=cFdCzN7RYbw

 Who do you most need to influence?

Think about your innovation idea.

- Who do you need on board? – write a list.
- Who is the key person? – prioritise them.
- Think a bit more about them – you could use the persona template that we used for customers in **Step 2** to help you get your thoughts organised.
- Look at the persona template on page 8 of the innovation toolkit: **www.thebusinessgym.net**

Having thought a bit more about the person you are trying to influence, in turn, work through what each of the above influencing tactics would look like if applied to them.

For example, liking: how do you get this person to like you? What do you know about them? Where can you find a common interest? If Dave in finance is the person that you need on board, let's say he has a picture of a pug dog on his desk. Then do some basic research on pug dogs so that you can hold a conversation with Dave about something that is important to him.

Do this exercise for each of the influencing tactics. Which is the one that you think will resonate best with the person you need to get on board? Now go and try it.

What's in it for me? Creating a win–win scenario

We all want to know 'what's in it for me?' When you ask people to get involved with your innovation idea, you could be asking them for many things: their time, money, expertise, or to back your idea and influence their peers. It's important that you consider what's in it for them before you approach them and really think about what they would want. For example, a 'what's in it for me?' might be the opportunity to work on a project that is high profile. This will be a win for someone wanting to climb the career path, but less so for the person who just wants a quiet life. So think about your approach and match it to the needs of the individual you are influencing.

You have to find a scenario that has something in it for you too. A true win–win scenario is not about a happy compromise, but a situation when both parties gain more by working together than by themselves. Below are some questions to consider when working through what a win–win scenario would look like:

- **Goals:** what do you want the end result to be? What do you think the other person wants?
- **What's in it for them?:** what are the benefits to them for getting involved? What are the benefits to you?
- **Trades:** what do you have that the other person doesn't – and vice versa?
- **Alternatives:** if you don't agree, what alternatives are there? How much does it matter if they do not come on board? And what alternatives might the other person have?

- **Relationships:** what is your relationship? Are there any hidden issues? How will you handle these?
- **Expected outcomes:** what outcome will others be expecting? What has the outcome been in the past, and what precedents have been set?
- **Consequences:** what are the consequences for you – and what are the consequences for the other person of being on board or not?
- **Power:** who controls resources? Who stands to lose the most if you don't agree? What power does the other person have to deliver what you want?
- **Possible solutions:** based on all of the considerations, what are the different solutions?

 **Win-wins**

Think specifically about the next priority person on your list that you need to get on board. It is likely that you need the support of more than one person.

Work through the above questions with them in mind.

List at least three different solutions. Then plot them on the win–win grid to help you check visually that they really are win–wins.

Now go and give it a go.

Examples of win–win scenarios

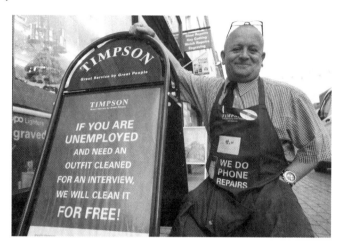

- Timpson, a UK shoe repair and key cutting chain, has two policies that create win–win situations. They help unemployed people by dry cleaning their outfits for job interviews for free. They also actively recruit ex-offenders and work with prisons across the UK to select and train new recruits. Free cleaning is a win for the job seeker, because showing up for interview in a clean suit gives a good impression and increases your chances of employment. It gives Timpson the opportunity to help people as well as being good for the Timpson brand image. Recruiting from prisons gives ex-offenders a second chance, helps them to find their feet and independence. For Timpson it's an effective way to recruit and train the staff they want. And of course both are excellent corporate social responsibility initiatives for Timpson.
- Interface, the world's leading designer and manufacturer of carpet tiles, teamed up with the Zoological Society of London to tackle the problem of discarded fishing nets damaging coral reefs and the communities that make their living from the marine and coastal ecosystems in developing countries. This partnership, called Net-Works, harvests the discarded nylon fishing nets from the reefs and uses the nylon for carpet tile production. Interface get a sustainable and profitable product,

the Zoological Society furthers its goal to protect marine ecosystems and the local community benefits from long term incentives to protect the natural resources that are needed to survive. In fact it is a win–win–win. To date, 61,845 kilograms of net have been collected.

- Marks and Spencer and Oxfam had a partnership where if you brought your M&S clothes into an Oxfam shop you received a voucher to spend at M&S if you spent over £35. This 'Shwopping' campaign was a win for Oxfam because it got more quality stock for its stores and a win for M&S as it drove more footfall and increased the spend of customers who were using a voucher.

In this step about not expecting anyone else to like your idea, the essential innovation principles to remember are:

- Involve other people with your ideas from the beginning of the process, both individually and through workshops.
- Use influencing techniques and win–win scenarios to make different approaches to people you need onside.
- Build your personal resilience. Remember: don't expect anyone to like your idea, and it may take several attempts to persuade someone to support it.

When you have tried the tactics in this step, you may also find the resources in **Skill 3**, innovating when no one else gets it, helpful.

Call to action

If you are reading this book step by step, before you move on to **Step 7**, have several different influencing tactics up your sleeve for specific people you want to get on board.

If you could take one idea from this step to practise in your day-to-day work, what would it be?

_____

_____

_____

Step 7

Filter and choose the best ideas

After reading this step you will learn how to:

- Employ some techniques to filter and choose the ideas to progress that have the greatest chance of success
- Discover which tools will help you make decisions on which ideas to progress
- Say a confident 'no' to the weaker ideas.

'Innovation is saying "no" to 1,000 ideas.'

Steve Jobs, co-founder and CEO of Apple

The story so far

In the last step you learned not to have an expectation that anyone will like your idea, and you are now armed with some ways to influence and get people on board. If you are working on a live innovation project you should be focused on the purpose of your innovation and have lots of ideas (including some crazy ones) about your innovation topic too.

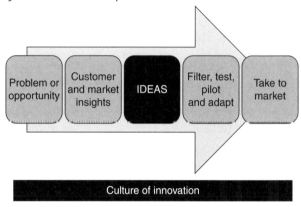

Steps for successful innovation

Filtering ideas

For many individuals and organisations the complexity of innovation really begins in making decisions about which ideas to progress and saying no to the ideas that won't help you achieve your goal.

If you have followed the steps in this book then it makes it easier to filter your ideas.

Strong project management skills are required throughout the whole innovation process, but they are absolutely essential from the point when ideas are filtered and progressed.

 You may already be really great at project management but if you have little experience or need a refresher, check:

www.businessballs.com/project.htm

for tips and templates that can help you.

In a workshop

If you have been generating ideas in a group (as described on **page 56),** at the end of the workshop it is helpful to cluster the ideas into themes, and ask people to vote on their top ideas.

A good way of doing it is to put the ideas on the wall, and ask people to vote with sticky dots. You could also give people first, second and third choices. This can give the group a sense of the ideas with the most support as well as signal to the group that they are an important and listened to part of the innovation decision process.

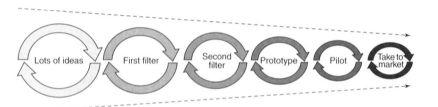

The innovation process

Filtering

The process of weeding out the weaker ideas to focus on the ideas that have the most potential to address your problem will depend on a number of factors, including the problem you set out to solve, the scope and scale of the idea, the resources available and the investment required to progress the idea.

Health warning

Every innovation idea is different so you need to take the principles and apply your common sense to the application of what is appropriate for you. Mix and match their criteria below and apply the principles to your situation. You can learn more about developing your own process and framework in **Part 3 on page 155.**

One-stage filter

If you do not have a huge volume of ideas, or need to move fast, or your organisation is small, or your idea does not require significant investment, a one-stage filter is probably your best option. Below is a simple checklist if you choose this route. Score out of 10 how your idea relates to each of the following. The idea or ideas with the highest scores have the most potential.

	Score
Strategic: does this idea address the original strategic challenge that was set?	
Insight: does your idea respond to the information you have about your audiences and the marketplace?	
Income: what potential does it have to make money once it is established (assuming this was part of your original criteria)?	
Brand: how well does the idea fit with your brand?	
Time: is your idea time specific, and if so is it achievable?	
Scale: is this an idea that can go big? Is it sustainable?	
Simple: how easy will it be to develop this idea and how much resource or expertise will be needed?	
Gut: what do your instincts tell you? Are you excited about your idea?	
For customers: what difference will it make for customers?	
Total	

 You can download the one-stage filter template on page 22 of the innovation toolkit:

www.thebusinessgym.net

Two or more filter stages

For bigger ideas or if you have lots of ideas, a two-stage filter process might be better for you. If so, the first filter is even more simple.

First simple filter

For any initial filter process first ensure, as above, that all the ideas meet the initial brief by asking the following questions of them:

- Does the idea address the innovation question/what the innovation sets out to do/problem or opportunity?
- What insight does it respond to?
- Can it be done?

Paul Sloane, innovation author/expert, recommends the FAN criteria at this stage. Are you a FAN of the idea?

- Is it Feasible?
- Is it Attractive?
- Is it Novel?

And retail giant, Tesco, uses the following criteria:

- Is it better? (For customers)
- Is it simpler? (For staff)
- Is it cheaper? (For Tesco)

Whichever criteria you choose (or you could develop your own based on your unique needs) the principle is that it has to be simple and it must answer the original innovation purpose you set out to solve.

 What are your three simple criteria for your first filter innovation? Write them down.

_____

_____

A second filter

You now have filtered out the ideas that didn't meet the initial criteria as well as some of the weaker ideas. That may be enough and leave you with sufficient strong ideas to develop. Or you may still have too many ideas to deal with in which case you now apply a more in-depth filter to make decisions on the remaining ideas.

Again there is no one right way of filtering, and you may choose to adapt your criteria depending on what you are developing ideas about, the resource available and investment needed. There is a balance of rational and intuition. Below are criteria to consider. Unless you are involved in product development this might be out of your remit, but understanding this part of the process will help you if you are in any way involved in developing ideas or if you are pitching your ideas to a senior manager, funder or someone responsible for product development.

1. Market

   - Size: what is the size of the current market, and what is the potential market share of your idea?

   - Growth: what is the current growth rate in the market? What is the likely potential growth in the future?

   - Appeal: what is appealing about entering this market? How much knowledge do you have on the industry involved?

2. Product

   - Uniqueness: how novel is your idea? What does it offer to the customer that is different from anything else in the marketplace?

   - Exclusivity (patentability): can you patent the product?

   - Scale: what is the scalable income potential of your idea? What is its geographical potential? How much would it cost to ship your idea?

   - Simplicity: how simple is your idea?

   - Lifespan: what is the potential of your idea? What is the shelf life of the product?

3. Feasibility

   - Product development: how easy is it to produce your product? How difficult is the design or business concept development of your idea?

   - Technology: what technology is required?

- Production: how will you produce your idea? How much effort is involved in the manufacture of your idea? How long will it take to get your idea to market?

- Personnel: who do you need and what skills will they need to produce it?

- Financial: how much money will it cost to implement? How long will it take to break even?

4. Fit

- Organisational infrastructure: what changes will you have to make to produce your idea?

- Personnel and managerial expertise: what skills gaps are there to develop this idea? Who currently on the team needs to be involved? Is there buy-in at the top level to support and back this idea?

- Marketing: how much marketing will your product require? Is your product a consumable?

- Sales: how easy is it to sell your product?

- Technical: what are the gaps in technology?

- Production: how much attention does your idea require? How complex is it to manufacture?

- Financial: what additional investment will be required?

- Customer/market needs: who are the customers? Are they current or new? What do you know about them? What is the earning profile of your potential consumers? How essential is your idea to the consumer?

5. Time

- How long will it take to develop your idea? What time commitment is required to develop the idea?

- How long before you need to make money from your idea?

6. Financial issues

- Investment requirements: how much investment will your idea require to prototype/pilot/take to market/scale? How expensive is your idea to start up?

- Costs: what is the cost to produce? Is your idea easy to distribute?

- Profitability: what is the financial potential of your idea? What is the potential profitability of your idea?

7. Other

- Gut feeling: do you have a gut feeling about your idea?

- Is it realistic? Hand on heart is this idea realistic?

- How committed are you to your idea?

8. Probability of success

- How risky is your idea? What are the reasons that your idea might fail?

Source: Taken from and developed from Cooper, R. G. (1988). The seven principles of the latest Stage-Gate method add up to a streamlined, new-product idea-to-launch process. Available at: <http://www.stage-gate.net/downloads/working_papers/wp_23.pdf>

You can download a template that will help you work through these questions. Fill it in for the idea you are working on. You can also go to www.ccdi.co.uk/rapid-idea-evaluator for more help to evaluate your current idea. This template can be used as a starting point to adapt for your specific needs.

Making decisions

The template might throw up further questions that you have to go and research to get more information about before making decisions on ideas to take forward. Also ideas should be viewed within product and market context, not in isolation.

Look at your other products and their performance, and also the offerings in your marketplace, so that you can see if your new idea fills a gap, or duplicates anything in your current offering or that of your competitors.

There are four well-known and well-used tools that can help you understand your product portfolio and understand new product development opportunities in the marketplace.

1. The BCG Growth Share Matrix: for understanding your product portfolio.

2. Ansoff Matrix: for understanding your portfolio of offerings in a market context.

3. SWOT and PEST analysis.

4. De Bono's Thinking Hats: making decisions based on six different categories.

 You can download templates for these tools and tips on how to use them in the innovation toolkit:

www.thebusinessgym.net

Decisions: yes, no or maybe?

The answer is not always a straightforward yes or no. The options that decision makers have are:

1. **Yes.** The idea has merit, meets all criteria and should move forward. The yes ideas are then categorised into:

   - **BAU:** feed the idea into 'business as usual' and implement.

   - **JDI:** 'Just do it!'

   - **JFDI!:** Do it fast! (You can work out that acronym).

   - **Own project:** this needs full planning and resourcing and needs to be a project in itself.

2. **No.** There must be a clear reason why the idea should not move forward.

3. **Adapt.** The idea has merit but in its current iteration does not fully meet the criteria. Modify or adapt and resubmit.

4. **Not yet.** If market conditions change then this idea may work. Hold for review.

Opportunity cost

You may need to rank your ideas to make decisions on which ones to prioritise. You have to be really brutal when choosing what ideas to take forward because every time you say yes to something, you're saying no to something else.

This is called opportunity cost: a benefit, profit, or value of something that must be given up to acquire or achieve something else. Since every resource (money, time, skills etc.) can be put to alternative uses, every action, choice, or decision has an associated opportunity cost. When choosing between two ideas, it can be helpful to determine the opportunity cost of picking one option over the other to see which would be the most beneficial option.

 You can download the opportunity cost decision template on page 23 of the innovation toolkit:

www.thebusinessgym.net

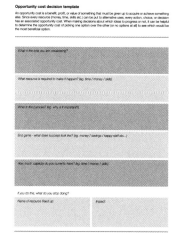

 Practical idea scenario

What are the opportunity costs?

This is a scenario based on a real situation. The purpose of this exercise is to help you think about a situation from a range of perspectives, explore the opportunity costs and also consider what further information you require to make an informed and final decision.

You work in a customer service centre and manage a team of 16 people. Your team responds to customer queries and complaints, primarily on the phone, by email and in the post, although there is an increasing amount of communication via social media. The majority of the team's work is reacting to enquiries that arrive between 9am and 5pm, although you are noticing increased demand outside of these times.

The company currently has a strict policy of 9am–5pm working hours that has been in place for many years. Your team work hard and are good at their jobs, but they complain regularly about the inflexibility of working hours when other local companies have a more flexible approach. In addition it makes journey times longer, as they travel in rush hour, as well as making it difficult and expensive to arrange childcare. Several members of the team have left over the past few months to go to competitors where they have more flexible working options, even though their offices are on a rather unpleasant industrial estate 10 miles further from the city centre. You fear that unless you make changes to working hours, more of your team will leave.

To find a solution to keeping your team happy by providing more flexible working that also meets your customers' needs, you ran a workshop with your team. Many ideas were discussed. The following ideas were assessed against criteria and are being considered.

Idea 1: maintain the core 9am–5pm policy and increase pay by 5 per cent. Develop an overtime policy to meet the needs of customers making enquiries outside of these hours.

Idea 2: trial shift working to offer employees flexibility to meet their needs, but which also meets the needs of customers around the peak times as well as the increase in 'out of hours' enquiries.

Idea 3: maintain the core 9am–5pm policy and trial working from home for up to half the week, with an option for paid overtime for increasing 'out of hours' enquiries. Investment in technology, such as laptops and data systems, would be required.

For each of the ideas consider the opportunity costs from your (the team manager's) point of view and then from the employee's point of view. Use the opportunity cost decision template and the persona template on of the innovation toolkit at **www .thebusinessgym.net** to help you.

The team manager's point of view

Idea 1: e.g. what budget can I take the 5 per cent increase from? It means we can't invest in new equipment this financial year.

_____

_____

Idea 2:

_____

_____

Idea 3:

_____

_____

The employee's point of view

Idea 1: e.g. pleased to be getting paid more, but flexibility would be worth more than 5 per cent in time saved.

_____

_____

Idea 2:

_____

_____

Idea 3:

_____

_____

What other information would you need in order to make a decision about which idea to test?

_____

_____

What are your thoughts and comments – which ideas would you consider, what additional information would you need?

_____

_____

Having ideas and filtering at the same time

So far we have talked about face-to-face idea sessions, conversations and decisions made in board meetings. There is idea management software that takes the human interaction out of this part of the process.

 You can look at the different options currently available at:

www.capterra.com/idea-management-software/

There are some organisations that are using web-based idea management software or crowdsourcing platforms to solicit, filter and select ideas from communities of their employees (and in some cases customers and partners). These crowdsourcing platforms post a time-limited strategic challenge to their communities, who submit their ideas for how to solve the challenge.

The community builds on ideas, votes them up (or down) and six weeks later (or however long the challenge runs for) the top 10 ideas are assessed against set criteria and either taken forward or rejected. The people who contributed to the winning idea are given the opportunity to work on its delivery. The benefit to this is that it can be used by anyone with an internet connection and a device, and while there are disadvantages to not getting people face to face there are advantages in opening up innovation to a global community. For example, Oxfam used this type of platform to think about how it could better use mobile technology and engaged and connected its employees, beneficiaries and volunteers across the globe. The project also gained awards for best internal communications that drove organisational change and increased efficiency.

The decision principles remain the same as earlier in this step, but given the slightly different process additional questions to bear in mind include:

- Does the innovation community support this idea?
- Did it receive a lot of interest through active conversation, voting or volunteering?

Who makes the decisions?

This depends on your organisation and process. In most cases the initial decisions are made by an innovation manager in conjunction with the people responsible for the strategic area that the ideas have been generated around. This is then presented as a business case to senior board level for sign off and investment. How you structure your innovation process (see **Part 3)** and idea decision making depends on your purpose, resources and expertise and an application of your own common sense. However, for any filtering and decision-making process to work effectively it must be standardised, transparent and be understood by all involved.

Once the decisions have been made

Saying no and keeping people on board

Innovation is both rational and emotional. We become attached to our own ideas and it is easy to start to make decisions based on emotion rather than rationale. With innovation there is never a 100 per cent guarantee that your idea will work; there will be an element of intuition and gut feeling in making decisions. However, when you are saying 'no' to people, bear in mind that you are not just rejecting an idea, you are rejecting something that they have potentially spent a lot of time and energy on and that they care deeply about. It can also take courage for people to speak up about a new idea, so rejecting ideas can be a delicate balance between being kind yet candid. Below are some tips to help you have the 'no' conversation and yet keep people on board:

- Always offer clear feedback on why ideas are not being progressed.
- Ensure the decision-making process is transparent and understood.
- Be to the point and respectful of how the person may feel about their rejected idea.
- Encourage them to stay involved – give specific feedback about the value they add to the process.
- Be candid and kind so the person is absolutely clear on where they stand. Refrain from your need to deliver a 'feedback sandwich' where you disguise the 'no' news between two pieces of positive feedback, which can give confusing and conflicting messages.

 The best way of learning is to practise. Work with a buddy and ask them to share their idea with you. Whatever their idea, use the above tips to role play and practise saying no to them.

Communicate

Regardless of the precise route you have taken, if you are working through this book step by step, you will have a selection of ideas that have been through a filtering process. It is not enough to make decisions and implement them, you must put plans in place to ensure that the decisions are communicated at the right level of detail to the different stakeholders that need to know.

One simple way to do this is to record them on a template so that every idea is recorded in the same format with the same level of detail. This serves as an internal document to communicate, get people excited about the idea and to provide you with a clear idea development record. You may want to craft your own, one that is specific to your organisational needs, but some information that is helpful includes:

1. Name of the product – this is really important. If you don't agree a name for the idea that everyone signs up to it runs the risk of being called many things and confusing everyone.

2. What it is in a sentence.

3. Why it's important to the organisation.

4. Why it's important to the customer.

5. What the barriers could be and how you can minimise them.

6. Visuals – draw it in action.

7. Competitors or related concepts.

8. Where this product is in the marketplace.

9. Criteria fit.

10. We love this idea because . . . .

 You can download the idea concept card on page 34 of the innovation toolkit at:

www.thebusinessgym.net

In this step about filtering and choosing the best ideas, the essential innovation principles to remember are:

- Combine the criteria guidelines with your own common sense to develop the best filtering process for your innovation ideas.
- Remember they are ruling principles not rules – do not underestimate your gut feeling.
- Be transparent about the ideas that are taken forward and the ones that are not, and always feed back to individuals who are involved and have submitted ideas.
- Develop templates that you can use to easily communicate and also get people excited about the ideas.

Call to action

If you are reading this book step by step, before you move on to **Step 8**, make a decision about one idea that you are going to take forward. It will help you get more out of the next step if you can apply it to a live idea.

If you could take one idea from this step to practise in your day-to-day work, what would it be?

_____

_____

_____

Step 8

Prototype, fail fast and refine

After reading this step you will learn how to:

- Understand prototyping and why it is an important part of the innovation process
- Discover practical ways to cheaply and quickly prototype your idea
- Map user journeys
- Gain feedback from colleagues, managers and customers to evaluate and refine your ideas.

'From cardboard and duct tape to ABS polycarbonate, it took 5,127 prototypes and 15 years to get it [cyclone technology] right.'

Sir James Dyson, entrepreneur

The story so far

If you have been following each step in order, you will now have chosen your strongest idea or ideas to develop, you will have a comprehensive understanding of the potential of your idea and now you will be considering taking it to the next stage.

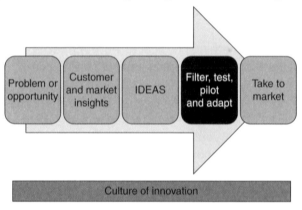

Steps for successful innovation

If you are not reading this book step by step and just dipping into this step, that's fine, but you will get more from it if you pick a real project to practise prototyping on.

Prototyping

A prototype is a sample or a model of your idea, whether it's a product, service or new technology. Prototyping is an important part of the innovation process because it:

- tests and refines the practicalities and functionality of your idea. Your idea works perfectly in theory, but it's not until you start physically creating it that you'll encounter flaws and then be able to fix them;
- tests the performance and suitability of various materials, for example, you think your new pin badge should be made from cheaper plastic, but when you prototype this, the plastic

can't be dyed to match your brand colours, so you have to reconsider;

- can help minimise risk of a product failing; because you prototyped you didn't order 10,000 off-colour pin badges;
- can help get buy-in from key stakeholders, including customers and potential business partners and funders. Seeing something helps bring your idea to life and helps others understand its potential in a way that a business case won't;
- can get attention; when you present or pitch with a physical object you separate yourself from the dozens of others who talk about their idea aided by another boring spreadsheet or PowerPoint;
- gives you something physical to work with, which encourages collaboration from potential partners and funders.

Have you ever sat and struggled to use something, follow instructions or even open the packaging? Are some services so frustrating to use you just want to give up? For example, I was recently in a coffee shop that advertises 'free Wi-Fi' as a benefit to customers. Laden with shopping bags I had to ask the barista how I accessed it, at which point he gave me a slither of paper with the access code on that blew off my coffee tray on my way to my seat. When I retrieved this scrap of paper, I had to peer at the code written on it in tiny font at arm's length to be able to see to enter it on my laptop (and it wasn't something simple like a recognisable word, it was a collision of numbers and letters – which took me three attempts to enter correctly). Then the login page informed me that the code lasts for 30 minutes! I looked around and there were no other people online. If the coffee shop had prototyped the process, or tested it with users, it might have been a much better experience.

Can you think of a time when your user experience could have been improved?

- What was it?
- What improvements would you make?

Case study

Protyping at PalmPilot

PalmPilot was the first computer hand-held device. It was invented in 1996 by entrepreneur Jeff Hawkins. The first prototype was a piece of wood, about the size of a deck of cards with a chopstick for a stylus and a printout taped to the front for an interface. Hawkins carried this with him in his pocket for weeks during which time he would 'use' it. Sometimes he would pretend to scrawl on the screen in meetings in an attempt to understand how his customers would use it. The development and launch of the successful product was credited to the prototyping approach.

User journey

Think about your idea from a user's perspective and imagine what their experience will be at each stage of the journey. There are five basic stages to a user journey lifecycle: aware, join, use, continue and exit. Consider how your idea will answer their need and how they will interact with it at different stages. Also consider how they move from stage to stage.

Split up the journey into five key phases and write down what happens at each stage:

1. **Aware:** the first step is how people are informed and learn about a new service.

2. **Join:** the first step in participating is to join. For example, this could be submitting an email to receive a newsletter or completing an application form for a gym membership.

3. **Use:** is when people use a service for the first time. This is often the stage at which people become frustrated when they are using a service they haven't used before.

4. **Continue:** is about how a person continues to use a service after the first time. It's when the relationship develops.

5. **Exit:** is the final stage when a customer decides to stop using a service. If the service is well designed they become advocates.

You can use this technique with your users, observe and record if it is a service role play and also map out the difference between what you want to happen and what actually happens to identify gaps.

Mapping the user journey will help you to you spot where the gaps are in your innovation. It also helps you understand what is required behind the scenes to make sure your idea works, e.g. people, resources, technology, etc.

 The storyboard on page 38 of the innovation toolkit that you can download from www.thebusinessgym.net is particularly helpful when exploring this technique. Use it to draw out stages and plot what needs to happen to get from stage to stage.

Storyboard example

This is an example of a completed storyboard, for a customer service helpline for a tech company. It might give you some inspiration for your storyboards

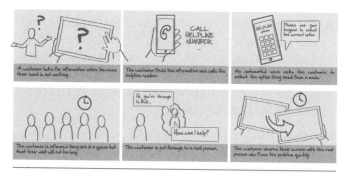

How to prototype

Prototyping is supposed to be quick, cheap and simple. Don't fuss over giving your prototypes a high gloss finish because you won't get honest answers from people if it looks like you've spent months developing them. The more unfinished they look the better, because it helps signal to people that the job is far from complete and encourages them to make improvements.

Below are a number of prototyping techniques that you can try.

Protyping techniques

Quick and dirty

Build your prototype using whatever comes to hand. Cardboard, sticky tape and marker pens are a prototyper's best friend (in fact get into the habit of collecting random items that you can use to prototype, like nuts and bolts, odd components, etc.). If you want to build gadgets and electronics from cardboard that's fine – the cardboard brings the prototype a roughness and allows the user to concentrate on the interaction.

Improvise, like the chopstick stylus in the PalmPilot! The ability to improvise saved the lives of the crew of the Apollo 13 when they had to fit a square peg in a round hole.

 www.youtube.com/watch?v=C2YZnTL596Q

With the items that you have on your desk, prototype your idea. Improvise with the materials you have.

Paper prototyping

When prototyping websites or apps it can be more cost and time efficient to sketch out the screens first before thinking about even talking to a developer.

Draw simple layouts of buttons and pictures on different screens and sit down with a user. If you can mock up a cardboard computer or smartphone it will add to the experience.

With no guidance at all ask your user to navigate through the sketched screens in the way that feels most natural to them. Depending on what button they push, put a different screen in front of them. This will give you valuable lessons about how you should build your website/app.

 You can see examples of sketch templates below and you can download your own sketch tool templates on pages 40–48 in the innovation toolkit from:

www.thebusinessgym.net

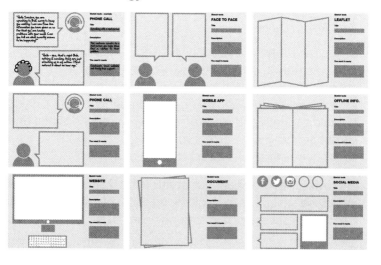

Role play

Assemble a team and in that team assume different roles as if you are users of your innovation. For example, your innovation might be a new coffee shop idea. Mock up the counter and service area and act out what will happen from a user's perspective by referring to your user journey (**page 87**) if you have created one. (You can also use role play to create your user journey as the different elements will become clear as you act it out.) Capture the key moments that cause tension or confusion. These are the areas that you must work through, because if they are an issue for you they almost certainly will be for your user too.

In the example on the next page, users were trying to understand the challenges drivers face when they drive in a platoon, driving in close proximity to save fuel and defeat air friction. How do they communicate about how much room to leave between the two vehicles and how do they understand each other's intentions? By role playing they can better experience and understand the situation and therefore uncover better solutions.

Bodystorming

Bodystorming is imagining what it would be like if the product existed and experiencing it by acting out your idea. It's about you moving and trying things out rather than imagining it in the abstract. It is important to understand and be your target audience as much as possible. For example, if your user has arthritis wear ski gloves to mimic how they might use a pen to pick something up or open something. If they have a visual impairment wear swimming goggles or dark glasses. If they have a problem with their hearing wear earmuffs. The insights you will gain from trying as much as possible to become your user will help to inform your design.

Asking for and listening to feedback

It is easy to fall in love with your idea and that makes it hard to be objective about the feedback that you receive. It's imperative that you listen and learn from the feedback of your prototyping because this will help you refine your idea or help you make decisions about what ideas to stop. Some tips to help you ask and listen for feedback are as follows:

- Don't *expect* anyone to like your idea (you already know this).
- Ask people what they think of your prototypes and allow them to speak freely. Don't try to influence answers.
- Don't be overly sensitive, you may not like or agree with the feedback. It is not for you to defend your idea, but simply to listen.
- Remember the feedback will help you refine your idea to make it better.
- Prototyping can also spark new ideas, so consider and test different solutions as people feed back. It is an iterative process.

Prototyping with customers

Your customers are also probably going to criticise your ideas, which is why it's invaluable to ask them. There are several ways you can do this:

- **Focus groups:** to test different idea concepts and prototypes with your target audience. Work with a specialist agency to recruit your audience and facilitate the groups. They will help to draw out what customers liked or didn't like about the idea, but also understand the reasons, as well as concrete points of reference to make improvements. You can get more from your focus group if you match the context to the environment, for example, for food related products hold the group in a kitchen, for a travel product in the resort, etc.
- **1:1 interviews:** you will get more in-depth and often confidential information in a 1:1 interview than in a focus group as people are inclined to be more candid in a 1:1 situation than in a group setting.
- **Panels:** many organisations will have a panel of their own customers, or work with agencies that supply consumer panels that have signed up to test products online.

Prototyping with internal teams

Internal teams will also be able to add valuable feedback. Throughout the innovation process you have learned that keeping internal teams informed and engaged will help you get your ideas to market. Prototyping is another way to engage with them. Some suggestions on how to do this are:

- Leave your prototypes in a place where colleagues can see them, encourage people to come and interact with them and give feedback.
- Hold a workshop for people you need on board to make and test the prototype.*
- If you are holding focus groups with customers also use it as an opportunity for employees to observe.
- Team meetings: can you take your prototypes to other team meetings or have a drop-in meeting each week/month for people to contribute feedback?

Choose whatever method will work for your organisation and make it part of your team's everyday work.

What tactics will you try? What other ideas do you have to prototype and get customers and colleagues involved?

Case study

Tackling the sceptics – the launch of the Sony Walkman

The Sony Walkman was launched on 21 June 1979. The concept of a portable tape player was new. At the time portable tape players were used by journalists to record interviews. The Sony Walkman was just for listening. It had no record button, so there was scepticism about its success.

Sony identified that in order for the Walkman to work Sony had to get the biggest sceptics, the journalists, bought in. They

---

*Note: with any workshops, even if people are not able to attend, it is still valuable that you invite them because you are sending the signal that their opinion and input are required and valued.

had to make the concept of going about daily life listening to a personal music system desirable for them.

Apparently Sony developed prototypes and instead of having a conventional product launch to the press, they invited the press on a bus tour. They hired actors to walk about in Tokyo posing with the Walkman while the reporters went past on their bus listening to a recorded tour on their Walkman prototypes.

Sony also distributed the Walkman to young people and celebrities around Japan, generating demand, and hired young people to walk through parts of Tokyo, offering passers-by the chance to listen to the excellent audio quality.

The prototype experience brought the value of the Walkman experience to life. A month after the Walkman became available in Japanese stores, it was sold out.

 Keep testing and never give up; you can learn more about prototyping from Dyson at:

www.youtube.com/watch?v=idpedDg_2ts

Evaluating your prototyping

What you do with the feedback on your prototype is critical. Moving beyond prototypes is the next step in the innovation process and is likely to involve significant investment of time and money so agreement on what the feedback means, and what the next stage is for your idea is important. Stopping an unsuccessful innovation at this point can be very valuable as it frees up resources to focus on a better bet. It is important that the next steps are agreed on. Questions to ask are:

- What idea did we prototype?
- What problem did it set out to solve?
- What are we going to change?
- Was anything unexpected?

- What was missing from our innovation?
- Recommendations – yes, no or adapt?

 You can download the prototype evaluation template on page 49 of the innovation toolkit:

www.thebusinessgym.net

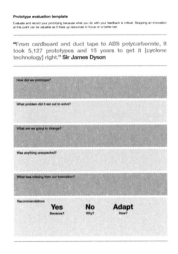

If your prototype gets the go-ahead the next stage is to pilot, develop and take it to market.

- Use different techniques to prototype your ideas as early as possible.
- Involve your colleagues and customers when prototyping.
- Be objective and really listen to feedback because this will help you improve your idea or make the decision to quit while you are ahead.
- Adapt and refine your idea based on feedback and record the process on a template – this will also help keep you focused on the end goal.
- Collect materials to use to prototype and bend your lateral thinking muscles to improvise with what is around you.

Call to action

If you are reading this book step by step, before you move on to **Step 9** use one of the prototype techniques on your idea. It will help you with the next step, and could even be fun.

If you could take one idea from this step to practise in your day-to-day work, what would it be?

In this step about prototyping, failing fast and refining, the essential innovation principles to remember are:

_____

_____

_____

Step 9

Pilot, adapt and invest

After reading this step you will learn how to:

- Design and deliver a pilot for your idea
- Evaluate so you know if it was successful or if it still needs finessing before you can take it to market
- Use tips to secure the resource to deliver your pilot.

'Intelligence is the ability to adapt to change.'

Stephen Hawking, theoretical physicist

The story so far

In the last step you did some prototyping. You might have ditched ideas, or refined them so you are confident your idea is ready to be tested in a live environment. That is exciting! Or you may just be reading to get a better idea of what a pilot is and how you do it.

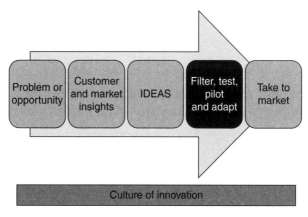

Steps for successful innovation

Piloting is about identifying and testing the minimum viable product **(that we spoke about on page 19 in Step 2).**

The minimum viable product or MVP is that version of a new product which allows a team to collect the maximum amount of validated learning about customers with the least effort.'

What your MVP is, will depend on the context of your idea. There are several ways your MVP can achieve least effort: with a small audience segment, for example 100 members of your target audience, or a narrower geographical area, like North London postcodes, or over a limited period of time, for example a month, or test interest through a crowdfunding platform.

Piloting builds on your prototyping to help you further mitigate risk, helps you to refine your plan, tests assumptions and gives you an opportunity to test different variables. Depending on what your idea or innovation is you could test price, audience, colour, time of day, etc.

It can also help you convince sceptics that your idea could work as they can try the product or process without committing, or see results that give a good indication of potential results.

 **Innovator's dilemma**

You're offered the chance to participate in two high-risk business ventures. Each costs £11,000. Each will be worth £1 million if all goes well. Each has just a 1 per cent chance of success. The mystery is that the ventures have very different expected pay-offs.

One of these opportunities is a poor investment: it costs £11,000 to get an expected pay-out of £10,000, which is 1 per cent of a million. Unless you take enormous pleasure in gambling, the venture makes no sense.

Strangely, the other opportunity, while still risky, is an excellent bet. With the same cost and the same chance of success, how could that be?

The answer is at the end of the book.

Source: Harford, T., 2014. Pilot schemes help ideas take off. BusinessDay, [online]. Available at: <http://www.bdlive.co.za/opinion/2014/10/22/pilot-schemes-help-ideas-take-off>

Using online to pilot

Online is a great way to test product development. Also referred to as rapid proposition testing, it allows you to find out quickly if your new idea appeals to your target audience. Here is a quick guide on how to do it.

- Create content by presenting your pilot as a consumer proposition, something that someone can 'buy'.
- Create an advertisement to recruit visitors to a website landing page. The advertisement can test between different products, or different creative/messaging. The landing page tests the ideas against each other.

- Drive traffic by using target demographics and key words to find the target audience, usually via paid advertising (e.g. Google AdWords) where consumers are responding to ads in a 'real world' environment.
- Track consumer behaviour by observing click-throughs and how people explore the pages.
- Analyse data using data captured from landing pages, and purchasing behaviour which could include:
  - o Winning/losing proposition – which is the strongest proposition?
  - o User demographics – who are your users?
  - o Device/browser usage – are people accessing on mobile, tablets or computers?
  - o Customer acquisition cost – what was the cost to get each customer?

In *The Lean Startup* by Eric Ries, the product is only manufactured/shipped if it sells online, saving materials, production and warehouse costs.

 You can read more about Lean Startup at:

http://theleanstartup.com

Piloting reduces risk and gives you the opportunity to adapt and refine – or choose to quit while you are ahead based on customer response. Consider the following examples:

- Outlier clothing that started with one pair of pants and a website. For the full story see founder Abe Burmeister at: **https://vimeo.com/41495120**
- Innocent Smoothies tested their original smoothie products at a festival and asked customers to vote on whether the founders should quit their day jobs to start their smoothie company. The customers voted yes.
- It's not just recent or technology enabled ideas that benefit from piloting. Marks & Spencer started out in 1884 when Michael Marks opened a stall at the Penny Bazaar in Kirkgate Market in Leeds.

What is your pilot?

- What is your idea?
- What is the minimum viable product?
- How will you pilot it?

Case study

Adapting to get products to market

SolarAid sells solar lights to communities in Africa at a fair market price through its social enterprise SunnyMoney. At the end of 2011, the team in Tanzania was attempting to replicate an approach they had piloted that had sold 3,000 solar lights in just three days on the tiny island of Mafia, near Zanzibar. The approach had used schools as the messenger. By communicating to teachers the value of solar lights, the message was passed onto children, who in turn told their parents. Mums and dads, motivated to help their sons and daughters study, bought their first solar light.

SolarAid used this approach on the mainland of Tanzania and its local teams arranged to go to schools and show them the solar lights. At first it didn't work. It took a lot of time to visit each school. Having failed, someone asked, 'What if we got all the head teachers together in one place?' This had two advantages: it was much more efficient, and who was the messenger now? Not a stranger from SolarAid/SunnyMoney – it was effectively the head teacher – one of the most respected people in the community.

SolarAid adapted its approach and worked with respected head teachers. It gathered them in one place to show them how solar lights are affordable (cheaper that the alternative, kerosene), and have health and educational benefits. In turn the head teachers influenced the teachers who educated the children who then inspired their parents to buy their first solar light. By the start of 2015, SolarAid had sold and distributed 1.5 million solar lights, becoming the biggest distributor in Africa, and is well on its way to achieving a goal to eradicate the kerosene lamp from Africa by 2020.

Measuring and evaluating your pilot

You need to be clear on what you are testing before you start your pilot so you know what success looks like. When evaluating the pilot, it's important to understand what influenced the success or failure. Was it an element of the product, or elements of the marketing – or a combination of both? A great idea could flop because of poor marketing or vice versa. It's important to be objective and clear on *why* your idea is or isn't working.

Once you have completed your pilot, you have to apply the same objectivity to its evaluation as you did to the evaluation of ideas and prototypes. Consider how it measures up against success criteria.

 Evaluation template

You can use the template in the innovation toolkit to evaluate your pilot, or simply ask the following questions:

- What happened?
- Is it what you expected?
- What will you change?
- What will it cost?
- Do it.

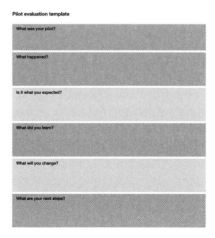

Pilot evaluation template

What was your pilot?

What happened?

Is it what you expected?

What did you learn?

What will you change?

What are your next steps?

You can download the pilot evaluation template on page 51 of the innovation toolkit at:

www.thebusinessgym.net

Pilot evaluation complete – what next?

There are four outcomes for your pilot.

1. **Yes:** Scale and roll out. Once you know your idea works on a small scale, you can replicate it on a large scale and take it to market.

2. **No:** Stop this idea now.

3. **Adapt:** The idea has merit but needs some adaptions. Make the adaptions and pilot again.

4. **Not yet:** If market conditions change then this idea may work. Hold for review.

Do you need investment for your pilot?

Whatever product or service you are developing, you will require resource. Whether, and when you pitch for resource will depend on your innovation process. There can be benefits for pitching for resource in two stages, for example to fund a pilot and then if successful the final product. It reduces risk for the investor and the successful pilot then forms the very tangible case for further investment. Whatever your process you will need to build the business case before you can secure any type of resource.

 You can download the business case template, which will help you summarise key areas, from page 52 in the innovation toolkit:

www.thebusinessgym.net

Key areas include:

- **The purpose**: or original problem this product/service solves.
- **The marketplace situation**: and why there is a need to do things differently.

- **How the future will be different**: if the organisation solves this problem.
- **Risk assessment**: if you have followed the steps in this book you have already minimised your risk at every step of the process. There are risks associated with new ideas as there are risks in continuing to do the same when the world is changing.
- **Opportunity cost**: show the risk of missed opportunities of not progressing your idea.
- **Measurement**: how you will know what a successful pilot looks like.
- **Finance**: required for the pilot: with an indication of finances required if the pilot is successful and you take the idea to scale (see Jargon buster, **page 209**).
- **Collaboration**: who you will work with to deliver, and if you have secured funding from elsewhere, add weight to your case by showing you already have support.
- **Delivery**: outline the pilot delivery, project plan, risks and operational details.
- **Project group**: who will be the core group of people to deliver the pilot.
- **Track record**: why you or your organisation are best placed to deliver this.
- **Make it real**: do whatever you can to bring the idea to life and show the difference it will make, for example bring your prototype to the pitch meeting.

Who are you asking for support?

You might be making a pitch to your manager, a senior team or external partners or investors. The business case asks all the questions that you need to answer to make a case for investment. If you do not require resource, you may just want to use the business case to help you develop your project plan for delivery. Also consider that whoever you are pitching to is a customer, and the same principles apply to them as in **Step 2**. Making a pitch for a pilot gives you the opportunity to find out more about your potential big investors. Work through the persona template and revisit the influencing skills that are outlined in **Step 6** to ensure you pitch in a way that appeals to them. Specifically consider:

- What is important to them?
- What is the difference they want to make?

 You can download the persona template on page 8 of the innovation toolkit at:

www.thebusinessgym.net

 Consider Don Draper's 'Carousel' pitch to Kodak in Season 1, Episode 13 of *Mad Men* (http://vimeo.com/20736616). What are your observations on tactics on this pitch?

Case study

How can we encourage active lifestyles?

Ramblers Scotland is a walking charity that exists to promote walking for fitness and pleasure and protect the places where people love to walk. Its initial GeoVation challenge pitch was just 100 words in answer to the question 'How can we encourage active lifestyles?' Its short and focused submission got it to GeoVation Camp in 2014.

Its idea that walkers would create a range of short walking routes in local communities was already working well on paper, but it wanted to make it easier for people by creating an app.

Ramblers Scotland's pitch to the GeoVation panel for investment for the 'Medal Routes App' was just three minutes with a maximum of six slides so it had to be concise, have absolute focus on the key messages that would resonate with the panel and cut out everything else.

After explaining the problem that the app solved, Ramblers Scotland focused on costs and income streams that the app could generate, for example advertising, to demonstrate sustainability after the funding ran out as well as measuring usage and effectiveness to show how the app was answering the initial challenge of supporting more active lifestyles.

Ramblers Scotland won £28,000 funding to develop the Medal Routes App. Through games and challenges, the app provides incentives to walk and map your own routes. It uses bronze, silver and gold level walks to categorise hundreds of walks at different levels of difficulty, all available at the swipe of your finger. It was launched in August 2014, just three months after winning the money, and at the time of writing had been downloaded over 4,500 times.

Source: Ramblers, Available at: <http://www.ramblers.org.uk/medalroutes>

GeoVation is an innovation around a challenge that involves geographical data as a key component. You can read more about GeoVation in **Challenge 3 (page 167)**.

In this step about piloting, adapting and investing, the essential innovation principles to remember are:

- Pilot your idea in a live environment.
- Build a business case and get investment for your pilot with a view to it being a two-stage process for further investment.
- Evaluate your pilot and then decide on next steps.

Call to action

If you are reading this book step by step, pilot your idea before you move on to **Step 10**, Take your ideas to market. Don't take something to market without piloting it first.

If you could take one idea from this step to practise in your day-to-day work, what would it be?

_____

_____

_____

Step **10**

Take your ideas to market

After reading this step you will learn how to:

- Develop your pilot to take it to scale in the marketplace
- Make a business case for investment
- Continuously monitor and develop your product and identify when to stop.

'It is not how many ideas you have. It's how many you make happen.'

Accenture advertisement

The story so far

If you have been following the steps in order you will be all set and ready to take your idea to market and if you have been dipping in and out, this step will give you some background on what's involved in taking an idea to market to help you prepare in the future.

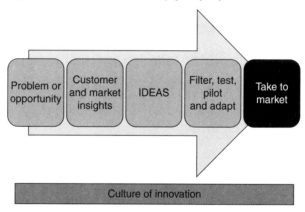

Steps for successful innovation

Getting the product into the marketplace is the final hurdle in the innovation process, but it is not the end. A constantly changing world means that you have to have a system for continuous improvement to ensure your idea remains competitive and current.

Scaling your idea

This is the process of taking your idea from your small-scale pilot and maximising reach and profits by taking it to a bigger customer base. First consider the conditions that you need to be ready to scale your idea. For example, it might be when all of the criteria are met: for example, 20 customers, each with a gross profit of £20 and all of them are satisfied or very satisfied with the product and service.

What are your indicators that you are ready to scale your idea?

When you are ready, an approach that makes scaling as simple as possible is the 1:10:100 ratio.

- The pilot is 1, which is the minimal work to pilot one product or service, e.g. supporting it manually or in a way that wouldn't be economically sustainable at scale.
- Then consider the minimum additional work to scale by 10, e.g. 10x more users, 10x more availability, 10x more clicks, etc. This helps you check to ensure the data from your pilot make sense for bigger numbers and helps you gain an understanding of what your technology or processes or systems or staff would need to do to achieve this increase.
- Then consider what would need to happen to scale from 10x to 100x. This figure might not be your full launch, you might still only be thinking of a region, or country or customer segment. However, taking this approach will help you think about what needs to happen to scale your idea.

 The template to help you scale ideas is on page 53 of the innovation toolkit at:

www.thebusinessgym.net

Using the 1:10:100 ratio – how will you take your idea to scale?

Business case to take to market

If you started the case for investment at the pilot stage you will now have more information to build a stronger and more detailed business case for investment to market. Or if you did not require resource for your pilot, this might be the first time that you are developing a business plan.

Your organisation or potential investor may already have standard investment requirements or templates. However, if you do not have one, your business case should include the following:

- **Idea and purpose:** what is the problem your idea is solving? Refer back to your original problem.
- **The marketplace situation:** why is there a need to do things differently?
- **Who benefits and how:** who are your customers and how will the future be different for them if you solve this problem?
- **Track record:** results from your pilot and track record of why you or your organisation are best placed to deliver it.
- **Delivery plan outline:** how you will deliver your idea or project plan, including operational details.
- **Resources:** how it will be financed and how it will be sustainable.
- **Risks:** what might go wrong and how you will mitigate against that.
- **Opportunity cost:** the cost of not progressing your idea.
- **Measurement:** how you will know what success looks like.
- **Collaboration:** who you will work with to deliver and if you have already secured funding from elsewhere, add weight by showing you already have support and a track record.
- **Project group:** who will be the core group of people to deliver the pilot, e.g. marketing, communications, sales, etc.
- **Make it real:** do whatever you can to bring the idea to life and show the difference it will make, for example bring your prototype and evidence from the pilot.
- **Continuous improvement:** how you will monitor and develop.

 You can download a business case template on page 52 of the innovation toolkit at:

    www.thebusinessgym.net

Case study

Liftshare

Liftshare is a social enterprise whose aim is to encourage sustainable transport options and cut carbon emissions by car sharing. Its challenge was to generate ideas to improve transport in Britain.

Liftshare's idea was a web-based personal travel planner (PTP) to provide people with the information they need to choose sustainable journey options.

Liftshare considered different ways to take PTP to market. The focus was on where it could make the most impact so it chose something that most people have to do regularly – the journey to work. Liftshare thought that the fastest and most effective route to market would be to work through big employers who could use PTP to provide their employees with access to a personal travel plan which included public transport, cycle routes and car share options. It also included information about sustainability, allowing people to make informed choices about the most convenient *and* sustainable option.

This was successful because it created a win–win situation. It helped employers implement their sustainability strategy while giving them the opportunity to help their employees get to work, and even saved money on hired car parking spaces as fewer people were using cars. It was good for employees as it gave them cheap and sustainable options to get to work and made car sharing easy.

Having successfully piloted this model Liftshare is now scaling PTP and working in partnership with 150 organisations including local authorities which are in turn offering PTP to their clients.

Innovation adoption lifecycle

Once you launch your product it will take time to gain traction. A typical innovation adoption lifecycle looks like this.

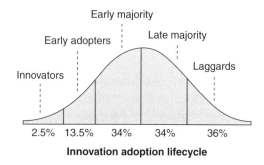

Innovation adoption lifecycle

Source: Rogers, E. M. (2003) *Diffusions of innovation*, 5th edition, Simon & Schuster

New products require time for adoption, since they usually require customers to become aware of the product and recognise its value. Usually there is a need by customers to test the concept, or see others test the concept, before the majority acquires the product. This is what author Geoffrey Moore called 'Crossing the chasm[10]'. This means your first adopters aren't the majority, and it will take a little time even for a good idea to enter the consciousness of the marketplace. So it can be difficult to assess whether your innovation has been successful for some time. Many consumer goods manufacturers for example give a product 6–9 months before making a decision whether to continue developing or to pull it. You must manage these expectations internally through good communication and relationships with everyone involved.

Continuous product development

Getting the product to market is a big achievement but you can't sit back and relax. You have to continually monitor your product performance and the marketplace. You need to keep up all the customer and market insight testing, evaluating and adapting habits that you used to develop your idea initially.

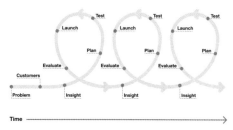

[10]Moore, G. A. (2014), *Crossing the Chasm*, 3rd edition, HarperBusiness.

Amazon is an example of an organisation which continually develops. Guided by an ethos of 'it's still day one' it has developed in new directions, from selling books to creating the Kindle to moving into the video-on-demand space.

An on-going understanding of your idea in the context of your current portfolio and the marketplace is important. When you understand how your idea and current portfolio are performing and meeting your audience needs, it helps you to spot opportunities to make improvements and also make decisions about what activities to stop doing.

Product lifecycle

Every product has a lifecycle, not all products will be relevant for ever – even the best ones. Monitoring product performance and deciding when you make the decision to stop is an important part of any innovation process. It could be when it ceases to be profitable, or before that if you start to notice a decline.

If you decide to stop or retire a product, consider the following questions:

- Why retire?
- Who does it affect?
- What alternatives do customers have? (Can *you* offer an alternative?)
- When do you plan product retirement?
- How do you communicate product retirement to customers?
- What is the competitor's position?

Record the reasons for the decision to retire a product and create a clear paper trail with all relevant information that can be accessed by relevant people in order to prevent reinvention (or re-launch!) of the product in question.

The following tools that are detailed in the innovation toolkit will help you continuously monitor your product portfolio and decision to retire or continue with a product:

- **The BCG Growth Share Matrix:** understanding your product portfolio.
- **Ansoff Matrix:** understanding your portfolio of offerings in market context.

- **SWOT and PEST analysis:** helping analysis of your products, internally in context of the marketplace as well as the broader environment.

- **De Bono's Thinking Hats:** making decisions based on six different categories.

In this step about taking your ideas to market, the essential innovation principles to remember are:

- Plan when and how you will take your product to market.
- Build a business case for sustainable investment.
- Develop a continuous loop for monitoring product performance and adapting if necessary.
- Consider your idea as part of an overall portfolio and in marketplace context.
- Have a system in place to signal when it is time to retire your idea.

Call to action

If you are reading this book step by step, well done! You will be familiar with all parts of an innovation process, and are hopefully well on your way to making your idea happen and are continuing to refine your innovation skills and knowledge.

If you could take one idea from this step to practise in your day-to-day work, what would it be?

_____

_____

_____

Every organisation is different, with different goals, resources, skills and experience. Innovation itself is not a linear process. If you are now keen to develop your own process or framework there is a summary in **Part 3 page 155** that will help you.

After reading **Part 1** you might also like to think about what sort of innovation collaborator type you are.

 You can find out by taking this quick test online in just three minutes:

www.100open.com/2013/06/what-kind-of-collaborator-are-you/

- What innovation collaborator type are you?
- What does this mean for you and your innovation?

Part 2

10 innovation skills in action

If you have worked through Part 1, you will have a broad understanding and experience of the vital elements of an innovation process and culture. Innovation is not a simple or linear process and you will encounter challenges and barriers at every step of the process.

This part and Part 3 will guide you through some common innovation situations. While you read these parts keep at the front of your mind three basic principles for successful innovation.

- **Purpose:** always be clear about why your idea or innovation is important: what problem does it solve or what opportunity does it exploit?

- **Insight:** use insights about your customers and the marketplace to inform your innovation ideas.

- **Comfort zone:** remember innovation can feel uncomfortable because it is about changing something, or testing something new or unknown. Accept that there is a degree of discomfort associated with innovation and practise working with that feeling.

No two innovation situations are identical so combine your own common sense with these principles to tackle your own, unique innovation situation.

Skill 1

Innovating in a big organisation

Do you ever feel like a small cog in a big wheel? That changing something is like turning a massive, slow tanker around? That what you do doesn't make a difference?

In a big organisation, whether its global with many regions and territories, national with multiple offices, or whether you work virtually or sit in the same office every day, whatever your role or position you can innovate in a big organisation. And to do that the first thing you have to work on is *you*.

You have choices about what you focus your innovation on in order to make maximum impact in a big organisation. You can:

1. Innovate within your current sphere of activity and influence.
2. Innovate outside your current sphere of activity and influence.

Your current sphere of activity and influence

You may feel that your organisation is so vast, or that because people work from many different locations the place where you can make the most impact is in your immediate role or team. If that is the case, choose and focus on an area that is within your control, for example:

- being more creative personally;
- increasing your knowledge and skills about something you are interested in or passionate about;
- focusing on incremental changes within your team; or
- developing insights from which you can make changes to your processes or services.

Using the steps in **Part 1** of this book focus on an area that you can do something about, that you don't need permission for and can commit to. Just start. Now.

Do something every day, no matter how small, to make your innovation a habit. Write it down. Note your progress. You will start to add more value because of the small changes you make. Other people will start to notice. As a result, your sphere of influence and activity will increase.

Outside your current sphere of activity and influence

If you feel bold enough, consider how you can work outside of your current sphere of activity and influence. First identify others who want to innovate and get them on board to work with you to make change happen. Identify the influencers in your organisation; the busy people who get things done. Who are the teams or departments that are most receptive to innovating? Who are the managers who can support you too? Don't tackle the whole organisation in one go, take small steps to get teams or departments on board one at a time. Have patience and resilience, innovation is a long-term strategy and it's not possible to make change happen overnight.

One tactic is to get a group together, and this is a good way of identifying the keenest innovators because they are the ones who will show up. Bringing a group together also positions you as the initiator, the go-to person for innovation.

Give people an incentive, a reason to get involved. Maybe it's an opportunity to get their problems solved, or to tackle a big strategic question, or simply a way to have fun and meet other like-minded people who want to drive change.

Case study

World Café

An effective way of doing this is through the World Café method. As the name suggests, the set-up is like a café with several tables of groups of people. It's both structured and informal. Each table has a host who facilitates a discussion around a specific question or topic. After a defined amount of time, usually about 10 minutes, the groups move to the next table and pick up on the conversation of the previous group. At the end, when all the groups have spent time with each host, the hosts feed back the total of all of the conversations that happened at their table. Success depends on slick organisation and thoughtful framing of the question about something that matters. Remember to use the 'How might we . . .?' question format outlined on **page 48.**

A UK auditing firm has used the World Café method successfully to develop ideas to solve client problems and encourage collaboration. While it took time to gain traction, word of the value of these sessions started to spread. The World Cafés were effective at getting people involved in ideas, participants had fun and the sessions had a buzz and energy to them. It highlighted the value of employees working with each other to solve problems and a business need for a more strategic approach to and investment in innovation.

 You can learn more about the World Café method at:
www.theworldcafe.com/method.html

Checklist

- Choose where you focus in order to make the most impact – either within or outside your sphere of influence.
- Be resilient – innovation can take time and it might not work first time.
- Just start something now.

Skill 2

Innovating on your own

Are you a team of one? Perhaps you are the only person working on a project? Or maybe you travel away from the office so often, you feel like you are working on your own?

For some, being autonomous is efficient because you can make quick decisions and move fast. However, more often, innovating on your own is hard because ideas spark off each other when people meet. Either way, if you are working on your own, you have to hold yourself to account for innovation. A way to do this is to be really strict about setting targets (e.g. set 20 minutes every day to focus on your innovation no matter what).

As a lone innovator you need to seek inspiration and connections to fuel your innovation ideas and delivery. Einstein said, 'We cannot solve our problems with the same thinking that created them.' One way to do this is to seek inspiration from outside your organisation.

Who else faces the same problems as you? It could be your competitors, or it could be further afield. If your problem is poor customer service, consider which companies are renowned for exceptional service. Perhaps you could learn from the First Direct case study featured on **page 21**? What could you learn from them, either by studying them or even picking up the phone to see if anyone can help? If the organisation is not a competitor there is every chance its people would talk to you.

The doctors at Great Ormond Street Hospital wanted to work faster as a team when taking babies from the ward to intensive care. They asked the Formula 1 team, who turn cars round in the pit stop in seconds, for advice. The teams at Great Ormond Street and Formula 1 worked together to apply the pit stop teamwork principles to the teams responsible for the transportation of seriously ill babies. The changes that they made resulted in more people being gathered round the beds when the babies were moved. To ensure more people being involved in the process didn't mean that they tripped each other up, the team at Great Ormond Street turned to another unlikely place for help. They consulted and learned from dance choreographers. The changes streamlined the process and reportedly reduced technical and information communication errors by 40 per cent.[11]

Sometimes the most unlikely partnerships have great results. For example, ask other people who are not close to your work for a fresh perspective, for example:

- People from different teams and departments – the less they know about the topic the better because they will ask questions that someone with knowledge of the topic would not think to ask.

- The new person who is yet to become part of the culture of 'how we do things here' – they too will have a different perspective.

- Your customers.

- Children, because they are experts in asking why? about pretty much everything!

- People from different industries – they may have had a similar problem in their sector that they have solved.

- People in different parts of the world who may have different problems and solutions.

---

[11] ASQ, Ferrari's Formula One handovers and handovers from surgery to intensive care. *ASQ* [online] Available at: <http://asq.org/healthcare-use/why-quality/great-ormond-street-hospital.html>

Case study

Southwest Airlines

Southwest Airlines has a reputation for innovation. Some years ago it ran a programme that included people from in-flight, ground, maintenance and dispatch operations. For six months they met for 10 hours a week, brainstorming ideas to address the broad issue: 'What are the highest-impact changes we can make to our aircraft operations?'

At the end of the six months the group presented 109 ideas to senior management, three of which involved sweeping operational changes. Chief Information Officer Tom Nealon said that the diversity of the people on the team was crucial, mentioning one director from the airline's schedule planning division in particular. The director had an almost naive perspective and his questions were so fundamental that they challenged the guys who had worked on operations for the last 30 years.

Source: Bloomberg, 2006. The world's most innovative companies. Bloomberg, [online]. Available at: <http://www.bloomberg.com/bw/stories/2006-04-23/the-worlds-most-innovative-companies>

Checklist

- Seek connections and inspiration to fuel innovation, look for where your problem has been solved by someone else.
- Consider the people least likely to be able to help you innovate and ask them for help.
- Be strict in holding yourself to account – spend 20 minutes every day. Just do it.

Skill 3

Innovating when no one else gets it

Have you ever felt that nobody else gets your idea? Do you ever feel you are explaining the same points over and over again like a stuck record? Or that people just don't really want to understand?

You have to start with managing your own expectations. Don't *expect* anyone else to get your idea, or if they do get it don't expect them to like it. If your idea is really new, *no one* is likely to get it. You have a lot of work to do to help them understand. In addition people tend to resist change, so anything that might involve them changing something, even if it's in their best interests, comes with a degree of apprehension. As an innovator it is your responsibility to help other people understand your idea. You have already learned some tactics to influence and get buy-in but here are some simple things you can do to increase your chances of that happening:

- **Start by picking your moment.** If the person that you want to get your idea works from a diary or schedule, then, make an appointment. Don't bound up to their desk brimming with enthusiasm for your great idea. If they are busy on something else you are unlikely to get a positive response.

- **Tell them what you want.** When you do introduce your idea be really clear what you want them to do with the idea. Do you just want someone to listen, or are you looking for them to build on it, or to challenge it?

- **Prepare for objections.** Think about what your idea means to the listener and the reasons they might not like it. Work out your answers for any negatives they might come back to you with, or questions they may have.

- **Push their buttons.** Think about what motivates *them*, what are the parts of the idea that they will like? How can you emphasise these?

Then tell them a story

Many of the world's best innovators and influencers are also some of the most accomplished storytellers. Martin Luther King used story in his 'I have a dream' speech at the start of the Civil Rights movement in America and Steve Jobs painted a story of his visionary future with his presentation that launched the iPad.

It is no wonder that storytelling is a key influencing skill. It is how human beings have shared knowledge and learning for centuries. We are hard wired to learn through stories, and scientists have shown that information learned through story provokes greater memory recall and connects us on an emotional level. Stories inspire people. For you as an innovator your ability to tell stories could be the difference between your innovation staying on the drawing board or making it to the marketplace.

Storytellers can describe problems and their solutions in a way that captivates attention and encourages action.

 Check out Nancy Duarte on the story structure of influential talks on TED:

www.ted.com/talks/nancy_duarte_the_secret_structure_of_great_talks

How to tell a story to get people behind your idea

There is a basic structure to any story. It goes like this . . .

1. **Set the scene** of the present situation, tell the listener who the story is about, give them enough information to make them care what happens. For example, Irene, who is too frail and frightened to leave her house after falling on some ice.

2. **Explain the problem.** The problem is that to pay her rent Irene has to go to the payment office in person. Irene is too frail.

3. **What does the solution look like?** If the payments could be automated (your idea), Irene could pay her rent easily without

the pain and expense of getting to the payment office and standing in a long queue.

4. **Paint the vision** of the bright future with the innovation complete and the difference it makes to people. Irene has less stress of having to struggle to the payment office and peace of mind that her rent is paid on time. Highlight how the listener has a role in making the better future happen by supporting your idea.

Once you have your structure, then consider how you tell your story to others. Below are some essentials:

- Make it about one person: people connect to stories of one person on an emotional level (e.g. Irene) rather than stories of the thousands of people like her.

- Make it simple, use simple language, no jargon or acronyms: your story has to be easily understood to be effective. A good litmus test is to consider if both your granny and a five year old will understand it.

- Think about your audience: what sort of story would appeal to their interests?

- It has to be real and you have to care about the story. If you don't care, you will not convince anyone else to care either.

If you have been following the steps in **Part 1** of this book you will already have a notebook or an online space where you are collecting ideas. Start to collect stories too, even if you just jot down a few words to start with. This will give you a choice of stories to tell the next time you need to influence.

Checklist

- Don't *expect* anyone to get or to like your idea.
- Pick your moment and be clear on what you want from the other person: to listen, build or challenge.
- Consider answers to objections as well as emphasise parts of the idea they will love.
- Tell stories about the better future your idea will create.

Skill 4

Innovating with your team

Is your team stuck doing the same activities and delivering the same results year after year after year? Does persuading your team to do something different seem like an impossible task? Can your day-to-day work be dull and unfocused?

It doesn't have to be like this.

'Team' can mean different things to different people in different contexts. The dictionary says that the verb team is *'to come together as a team to achieve a common goal'*. What does team mean to you? Who is your team? Is it your co-workers who work in the same part of the organisation as you? Is it the people who sit near you? Or do you view your friends and family as your team who support you in your life to achieve your common goals? A team can mean any or all of these things.

Whoever your team is, the first step to innovating with them is to find their shared purpose: the common goal that they can work together to achieve.

Let's consider team in a work context. You could find your common goal by referring to the team strategic plan, or key performance indicators (KPIs) or the organisational strategy. You might come up with some common goals to increase sales by 5 per cent this financial year, or to launch a new product, or to increase income from new customers by 10 per cent.

This is fine if you are looking to just make incremental changes, but if you want to make big change you need to throw the strategic plan away and create a burning platform. A burning platform is a potential crisis that could happen. What if the worst did happen? What would that look like? Perhaps your competitor released a product that put you out of business, or the cost of an essential raw material quadrupled overnight, or the finances were miscalculated so the predicted profit from the current business model is actually a loss. Make the crisis relevant to the team. Then make it feel real, for example sending the crisis news as an official email, or mocking up the front page of a newspaper with a crisis headline. By creating a burning platform you force a situation where doing the same activities that you did last year is not an option. With your burning platform ignited, what would you need to do differently? Now together, set your bigger, bolder common goal or purpose.

Deciding the shared goal together as a team is important, we are more likely to commit to and be accountable for goals that we have created ourselves.

High-performing teams also revisit their goals periodically as a way of reinforcing their commitment amongst themselves as well as checking that their common purpose is still relevant.

When the team is committed and clear on its shared goal it makes it easier to say yes to activities that get them closer to achieving it and say no to the activities that won't. It also lessens conflict, because the only thing the team should disagree on is *how* to achieve its common goal, for example challenging each other's assumptions, or different possible solutions in the hope of arriving at a better answer.

Make it happen

You have agreed your common goal together, how does that play out in your day-to-day team working? How do you make it happen? Here are some tactics that you can use:

- **Make it visible:** write the goal somewhere where everyone sees it, so people are reminded of and grounded back to their common goal every day.
- **Revisit it periodically:** to check that you are all still aligned and your common goal is the right focus.

- **Challenge:** get into the habit of asking the question of yourself and your team, 'Will this innovation activity get us nearer to achieving our common goal?'

- **Start your team meetings with the common goal:** for example, John Stewart, the Chairman at Guide Dogs for the Blind, starts his meetings with 'There are 180,000 people in the world that can't see, our job in this meeting is to make life better for them.'

- **Get out more:** have meetings somewhere different. I don't mean from meeting room 3 to meeting room 4. Get outside, go somewhere that relates to your common goal, which can inspire and provoke different thinking.

- **Time:** together allow time to focus on innovation. Whether it is a day a week, or a day a month, find a way to make dedicated time.

- **Inspire each other:** share ideas, inspiration, things from outside the team that can spark ideas like you did in **Step 4.**

- **Find an irritant:** sometimes, it can help to send in an outsider with a defined remit to challenge. It can highlight strategies that the team overlooks because they are too close to the subject. Some teams even benefit from employment of a full-time irritant to mix up the team dynamic and help challenge assumptions.

Case study

The irritant

At an ideation session with a large consumer packaging goods company, a senior member of the research and development organisation showed up to play the role of the irritant. Unlike the rest of his colleagues who came in standard business casual dress, he wore a bright bow tie and jeans. He spent much of the day bouncing ideas off other colleagues while also reacting to and building on the ideas of the group. While his comments were imaginative and relevant, they were far from succinct and he didn't seem bounded by the agenda. At the end of the session, however, the room was buzzing with a handful of insights that this man had contributed. His ability to think expansively, his long history working with and studying corporate innovations and his confidence to think out loud while stumbling into the next great thought allowed him to add significant value.

Checklist

- As a team find your common goal.
- Choose whether to make incremental changes or create a burning platform.
- Find ways to keep regularly focused on innovation.

Skill 5

Innovating with clients and customers

Have you ever had a great idea but lacked the skills or networks to make it happen? Could you develop better ideas and bring them to life if you worked with people outside of your team? Do you fear taking the sole responsibility of an expensive innovation failure?

Innovating with individuals and companies from outside your organisation and sharing the risks and rewards that go with that is called open innovation. *'Because not all the smart people work for you,'* as Bill Joy, co-founder of Sun Microsystems noted.

There are risks associated with any innovation, because something that is new is not guaranteed to work. Typically fewer than 1 in 100 new ideas ever make any return. Innovation can also account for up to 15 per cent of turnover.

Open innovation sources ideas from diverse perspectives and different knowledge and skill sets, and in particular, involving customers in the development of products and services has been shown to reduce risk.

Case study

Open innovation

Procter & Gamble embarked on its open innovation programme called Connect and Develop as early as 2001, collaborating with individuals and companies around the world to develop innovative ideas and products. At that time less than 10 per cent of its new initiatives involved external innovation partnerships. The company set a goal to increase this to more than 50 per cent. By 2008, that target had been smashed and Connect and Develop had become a fundamental part of business within P&G.

How to do open innovation

Innovating with others means opening up to the fact that you don't have all the answers yourself.

We often feel that we fail if we are not able to come up with a solution ourselves, but it is only when you ask for help that you give people the opportunity to build ideas with you. Sometimes it involves letting go of your ego in order to ask for help. Often others are delighted to be asked for their ideas and opinions, and this in itself is a good way of building relationships. Consider who you could partner with for open innovation, for example:

- an organisation or person that has already solved your problem;
- an organisation or person that is trying to solve the same problem;
- an organisation or a person that has the skills, experience or networks to help you realise your idea;
- customers who want better products, services or experiences.

Four simple steps to open innovation

1. **Pinpoint the purpose:** like any other innovation, open innovation starts with identifying a problem, opportunity or an unmet need.

2. **Find partners:** there are two common options for seeking open innovation partners.

   - Publish a challenge or brief to the outside world to encourage individuals and organisations to respond.

   - You already have your idea but need a partner with different attributes to you to make it happen, so you simply approach them. For example, you might need expertise in logistics and a distribution network to make your idea work, so you would look for partners that specialise in logistics, for example the Post Office, Amazon or Coca-Cola (also see **Step 5**).

3. **Agree on a shared purpose:** what is the win–win scenario for all parties (open innovation can involve multiple partners)?

4. **Co-develop:** together with partners co-develop innovations, in the same way as you would with any other innovation process. The most promising are then piloted and brought to market

through a variety of collaborative business models (e.g. licence deals, joint ventures or acquisitions).

Rewards

Rewards for open innovation are monetary but there are intrinsic rewards too. People are motivated by the satisfaction of solving a problem, or to gain profile, to learn something new or a career progression. Rewards could be:

- a prize for individuals, for example cash prize or support to make the idea a reality;
- a percentage of sales revenue;
- the pure satisfaction of seeing your idea on the shelves.

Case study

Customer-led open innovation at LEGO

In 2003 LEGO was on the verge of bankruptcy, faced with growing competition from online games, and possessing an old-fashioned brand image, LEGO turned to open innovation as one growth strategy to turn around the failing business.

One example of how LEGO utilised open innovation to drive growth is LEGO CUUSOO. First tested in Japan in 2008 this crowdsourcing platform invited anyone to post new LEGO design ideas, within a criteria framework that included conforming with brand guidelines and using only existing bricks (no new brick designs were allowed). If the idea received 10,000+ votes within a year then LEGO committed to producing the product and the originator of the idea received 1 per cent of the revenue.

LEGO CUUSOO exceeded expectations in terms of sales, largely due to customer involvement. It also led to a lucrative partnership with popular online game *Minecraft*. The CUUSOO community had over 500,000 members which evolved in 2014 into the crowdsourcing site *LEGO Ideas*. The LEGO ideas platform has already facilitated new niche products to market, including *Back to the Future*'s DeLorean and the *Ghostbusters'* Ectomobile.

For LEGO, this approach has had many benefits. It has solved the question before production of 'Will anyone want to buy this?', and diversified its customer base – adults are buying LEGO for themselves, not for their children. It has built a huge degree of trust, engagement and loyalty with its customer community. LEGO is not only bringing its customers' wishes to life but rewarding them with a percentage of profits too!

 Check out LEGO ideas at:
https://ideas.lego.com

Checklist

- Be clear on the shared purpose of what you will innovate about.
- Build networks of potential partners and be bold enough to approach them.
- Co-develop win–win ideas and business models.

 If you are interested in developing your open innovation skills check out the open innovation toolkit which is free to download courtesy of 100% Open, which worked closely with LEGO Ideas, at:

www.toolkit.100open.com/#about-the-toolkit-jump

Skill 6

Innovating your managers

Would your manager rather stick to what they know than take a risk and make a change? Or have you had to manage an over-enthusiastic manager who expects everything delivered today? Perhaps it's always a struggle to convince your manager to give your idea a go?

Your manager will have many of the same hopes, dreams and fears as you around innovation. The principle for managing up is about helping your manager manage you, while you help them to succeed.

The secret is to establish a mutually beneficial partnership where you are a resource for each other. Ways to achieve this are:

- **First understand them:** your manager, in an innovation context, is your customer. Apply the principles of understanding your customer that you learned earlier (in **Step 2**) to them. Get to know them, understand their strengths and weaknesses and the things that keep them awake at night.

- **Align goals at the start:** agree with your manager the purpose of innovation and their expectations, goals and timelines.

- **Common language:** a common language is critical for communicating around innovation. I've seen many managers and teams using different words to describe the same things, and they felt like they were disagreeing with each other which caused needless friction when actually they were in agreement but just using different words. Agree the language that you will use to describe innovation. The jargon buster at the end of the book may help you.

- **Style:** when you're managing up, you're managing the way your manager wants to be managed, not the way you want to be managed, so their style might not match yours and it might feel uncomfortable. Learn to match your communication style with that of your managers when on the phone, in emails and in person. Understand their communication preferences: do they want stacks of detail or just top line items? Would they prefer you just get on and tell them what happens at the end or do they want to know progress every step of the way? When you know what they prefer, you can adapt your communication style, which will help you to build a trusting relationship.

- **Make them look good:** part of your role is to help your manager succeed at innovation. Meet their needs, pre-empt and provide the information they will need for *their* managers.

- **Choose your battles:** keep the small problems away from them, take responsibility and where you can, present them with solutions not problems. This is a time when it is OK to be solution focused.

- **Involve them:** and help them think it is their idea. Prepare them with both successes and failures before everyone else. Be candid about failure. Tell it exactly as it is. Do not downplay it.

Taking all of the above into account, if you don't make progress, it's time to consider how important your innovation is. If it is going to get you nearer to your goal, it is your job to make it happen, and if that is the case it may be necessary to seek forgiveness over permission and operate in stealth mode. This means that you need to prototype and pilot your idea, show the data that prove it will work, and show how developing this will help your manager look good and achieve their objectives.

Over enthusiastic

What if you have the opposite problem that your manager is totally aligned with the purpose but wants everything delivered yesterday? Research shows it can take anything from 12 to 33 months from initial concept to product launch, yet most people have no clue that it will take more than a few months. This can often lead to tension. Here are some ways to manage this:

- Understand your manager's pressures. Find out why this idea has to be delivered yesterday. Where is their pressure coming from? If you know where their pressure comes from you can work with them to find alternative solutions.

- Don't take it personally: their need for speed is unlikely to be about you not delivering something, but a situation that is outside your control.
- Refer back to the agreed process and explain why it is taking longer than they anticipated. If you are on the agreed schedule explain why the stages are important, for example to minimise risk.
- Is it feasible to do things more quickly? What would that look like? What would you have to stop doing, and what would the impact of that be?
- Follow up any conversations with an email or written confirmation to help clarify that you both have the same understanding.

The other common managing-up challenge for innovators is that the chief executive or someone really senior has an idea that they think is great and so asks the organisation to develop it. Because someone important has had the idea often people disregard any process and jump to deliver a potentially duff idea, wasting a lot of time and resource. This can be really tricky to deal with. Here are some suggestions on how to tackle this situation:

- Assess the idea against your innovation framework. If this is an idea that meets the purpose and is strategic or provides an opportunity it goes through the process like any other idea.
- If the idea does not meet the purpose, be absolutely candid and explain why the idea isn't going be progressed. Use the rationale for the innovation process that they will have agreed to as your starting point.
- Highlight the things that would have to stop in order to deliver this idea.
- Ensure you communicate early with anyone who might be asked to deliver the idea directly to stop them downing tools and jumping to do what the boss says. A clear communication programme that complements your innovation process will also help to ensure that rogue ideas suggested by the boss don't make it under the radar.

Finally, refer to tips for saying no on **page 80**.

Checklist

- It's your job to make your manager look good.
- Understand each other and adapt your styles.
- Be candid about failure and practise saying no.

Skill 7

Innovating with confidence

Have you ever felt uncertain that your idea was going to work? Or out of your depth convincing others about the potential of your idea? Are you as confident as you would like to be about your innovation?

Remember that we all have times when we feel uncertain or lack confidence, and we feel this even more frequently when we are deliberately pushing ourselves to do something new or unknown. This means that innovation is a hotbed for crashes of confidence. Confident people inspire confidence in others, and successful innovators actively work on their own confidence as an ongoing part of their innovation process.

The good news is that becoming more confident in innovation, with focus and determination, is readily achievable. The following 12 steps will help you.

1. **You are already great:** Take stock of what you have already achieved – it might be feedback from a manager, a thank you from a customer or the time you delivered an excellent project. Create a confidence diary and write these achievements down. Look at your list to remind yourself of how great you already are and be appreciative of the opportunities you have realised. Keep writing down your achievements as you accomplish more. Look at this list regularly. When you have a moment of low confidence, refer back to this list to boost your confidence back up.

2. **Consider your strengths:** What innovation skills are you good at? Then consider the areas you want to improve on. Set yourself innovation goals. Make them SMART. What is it

that you want to achieve and by when? Know what success looks like and write it down, for example, 'I would like to have prototyped three ideas by the end of Q1'. Once you have set your goals, then decide on the small steps you need to take to achieve them. Now start. With each small step you achieve on your way to your goal, write it down in your confidence diary, celebrate it and move onto the next one.

3. **Stretch your comfort zone:** Build your confidence by taking small steps that stretch you outside of your comfort zone. You know when you are stretching yourself because it will feel a bit uncomfortable. For example, if your first step was to make an idea presentation to your team, can you now stretch to the next step to present to a team that you don't know well? Gradually expand comfort zone with each small step. This will help to grow your confidence and over time enable you to take on braver and bolder activities.

4. **Handle failure:** Failure in innovation is inevitable. It doesn't matter that you failed. What matters is how you dust yourself off, learn what didn't work, bounce back and give it another try. Everyone experiences setbacks, but not everyone gets back up. It's the getting back up that builds confidence, and you've got to fail in the first place to give yourself the opportunity to do so.

5. **Manage negative feelings:** We all have negative thoughts that eat away at our confidence. It's normal. Confidence is about learning to manage those thoughts that don't necessarily represent objective reality. When you experience those negative thoughts question them by reaffirming to yourself:

- I am choosing to do this because . . . (why this activity is more important than the fear).

- What is the benefit that I want to come from this (what is the positive outcome you want)?

- What is a more useful way of framing this fear (acknowledge that it is fear because the task you are doing is important – then focus on how you will achieve it)?

Another way to manage those negative feelings is to visualise yourself succeeding, for example imagine yourself delivering a winning innovation pitch. This helps you to feel more confident in the present moment. Practise visualising your success for the part of the innovation process that you feel least confident about, and you will be able to more easily conjure up confidence when you need it most.

6. **You are a change maker** As an innovator you will run into opposition, questions and doubts, because you are challenging the status quo and driving change. That doesn't mean you should ignore warning signs, but it does mean you should expect negatives, put them in perspective and prepare answers to overcome the objections.

7. **Find a mentor** There will be others who have been through what you are going through who can help build your confidence. Seek them out for their advice. There is advice on how to do this in the mentor section on **page 200.**

8. **Surround yourself with confident companions** Hang out with people who help boost your confidence. Find trusted companions to work with on your innovation ideas who will both challenge and support you.

9. **Do your homework** Good preparation can help boost your confidence, for example, if you are working on a presentation, practise it, ask for feedback, make changes and then keep practising.

10. **Look after yourself** Your health and wellbeing have a positive effect on your mood, effectiveness and confidence. Take regular exercise and choose a nutritious diet.

11. **Fake it until you make it** When you are not feeling confident pretend that you are. Stand tall, keep your shoulders back, your spine straight and your chin high. Breathe slowly and deeply. When you look like a confident person on the outside, you'll be approached as one by the world around you. You will fool other people and you'll fool yourself too.

12. **It's OK to ask for help** It is not weakness to not know the answer; it is a strength to be honest about your limitations. Ask other people for help. The worst that can happen is that someone says no, and then you can just ask someone else.

Over-confident vs under-confident

Most people struggle with under-confidence rather than over-confidence. The secret is about balance. Over-confidence can be as destructive as under-confidence. If you are under-confident, you'll avoid taking risks and stretching yourself, and you might not try at all. And if you're over-confident, you may take on too much risk, stretch yourself beyond your capabilities, and crash badly.

With the right amount of confidence, you will take informed risks and stretch yourself (but not beyond your abilities).

Checklist

- Write down your achievements and refer to them when your confidence dips.
- Focus on goals that take you outside of your comfort zone.
- Manage negative feelings and failure.
- Fake it until you make it.

Innovating by imitation

Do you think you will get found out if you don't come up with a completely original idea? Worried that it's bad form to replicate something that already exists? Or think it's a creativity cop out to replicate someone else's idea?

Stop worrying. Human beings have been copying, imitating and stealing each other's ideas since we lived in caves. The human race has progressed and evolved by imitating and improving on each other's previous ideas.

In today's business world it happens across all sectors. Zuckerberg didn't invent social networking: Friendster launched in 2002, Myspace and LinkedIn in 2003. Facebook didn't come along until 2004 as a Harvard-only exercise before being launched to the general public in 2006. Ryanair copied the budget airline model pioneered by Southwest Airlines, Asda took its high volume cheap prices model from Walmart, and finally even Steve Jobs cobbled together the original Macintosh user interface out of ideas and technology he previously encountered at Xerox PARC.

It's OK. In fact it is more than OK. Some of these copycat businesses became successful with the blessing of, and some even secured financial backing from, the original business founders.

Imitation is not just mindless repetition; intelligent imitation is taking an idea and applying it to your market and your context. It is doing what someone else has done, only better, cheaper and faster with an added sprinkle of your own originality.

Research by Oded Shenkar, a professor of management and human resources at Ohio State University who wrote the book

Copycats: how smart companies use imitation to gain a strategic edge, claims that typically, the better returns go to business people often disparaged as copycats. When imitators execute well, they usually succeed better than the first movers, because they study the errors of the innovators and learn from them, for example in the same way Facebook learned from the mistakes of Myspace.

Shenkar also highlights examples of companies that innovated new products but later lost out to others who imitated them. For example, Diners Club created credit cards but lost the market to MasterCard and Visa; EMI created CAT scans but the market today is dominated by General Electric.

An innovation strategy of imitation

It is perfectly legitimate to choose to make your innovation strategy based on copying other people's ideas. In fact it is a principal tactic for creating niche product innovation. It can also reduce risk by replicating something that has been tested already. There are four key ways that you can focus your innovation by imitation. They are not mutually exclusive, you can mix them together for great results too:

1. Take lessons from one market sector and apply them in a new way to your sector. Zipcar took the car rental market and made it relevant to the city motorist.

2. Build on an existing innovation and make it specific to your market. Amazon took the iTunes model to the book industry and introduced the one-click payment method.

3. Build on an existing innovation and make it better. Google took an existing idea for an effective search and made it better through the application of ranking factors.

4. Apply innovation to the process rather than the product. Henry Ford changed the way cars were built by using a moving assembly line. He took the idea from the meat processing industry.

How to innovate by imitation

- Actively search for ideas worth copying. Look outside and far away from your industry or sector. Ask a 'How would . . . ?' question to spark some ideas of where to look for inspiration. For example, if you want to innovate around increasing repeat business in your furniture retail business, think, 'How would a catering company approach this, or a construction firm, or a fashion company or a dentist?'
- Don't just copy an idea, seek to make it cheaper, better, faster, different or a combination of all of these things for both you and for your customer.
- Timing is everything, so you need to get to market when competitors are few and margins are still attractive. In some industries where there are few set-up costs it is relatively easy to imitate quickly and the products can be copied fast, for example the garment industry where high street chains have the imitations of the latest designer collections in store within hours of them leaving the catwalk. However, getting to market at the right time is harder when set-up costs are high and to imitate requires significant research and development.

Health warning

One health warning when copying is if in doubt to seek legal advice. Samsung and Apple have been battling more than 40 patent lawsuits and have jointly spent more than $1 billion in the past four years trying to prove that one poached the other's smartphone technology.

Checklist

- Imitation can be an effective strategy for innovation.
- There is no shame in imitation – steal with pride – but take care you don't infringe patent or copyright law.
- Don't just copy – make it cheaper, faster, better and different for you and your customer.

Innovation with no budget

Is securing a budget for innovation an impossible task? Are you expected to keep delivering more for less? Do cuts and efficiencies impact on what you are expected to deliver?

It is a myth that you need big budgets to be good at innovation. In fact shortage is a major innovation driver. With no money you have to force yourself to be more innovative. Your biggest resource is your own and your team's ingenuity and then your determination and resilience to do whatever it takes to make your ideas happen.

There are many organisations with abundant resource for innovation and this acts as a comfort cushion. Innovators with big budgets can lack urgency and passion and ideas easily get stuck in bureaucratic sign-off processes. Take a look at successful entrepreneurs and start-ups, many of which make their ideas happen on a shoestring.

If, for whatever reason you have no budget, don't waste your energy complaining about what you don't have. Focus on what you do have and strategies to get what you need and your ideas realised. Become resourceful and improvise. Below are some suggestions:

- **Connect back to the purpose of your innovation:** remind yourself why this innovation is important. It is only when something is important that you will make it happen.
- **Step up or step out:** if you can't find something meaningful to innovate about that inspires you then just quit now.
- **Find partners:** you can work with who bring resource, money, skills and technology.

- **Focus on incremental innovation:** focus on small incremental changes that you can just implement without any sign-off or process, permission or budget – the aggregate of these add up to make a difference.
- **Look for volunteers:** find other people who will volunteer to help you. This might be in your team, students seeking experience for theses or dissertations, or someone seeking work experience or change sectors.
- **Get really good at prioritising:** with limited resource you are forced to prioritise on the work that matters. Ruthlessly focus only on the activity that will get you closest to achieving your purpose.
- **Up-skill your colleagues and internal teams:** equip them with skills in creativity, idea generation, insight gathering and developing ideas. Many organisations with limited resource train internal innovation champions which also helps to embed a culture of innovation.
- **Involve customers:** be alert to their needs and wants and involve them in creating and developing ideas.
- **Think creatively:** about internal teams that would sponsor your innovation, for example if you are up-skilling internal teams and encouraging collaboration then HR may have budget to support this because those outputs and benefits are often be part of their remit.
- **Secure a sponsor:** think creatively about who would sponsor or fund your idea, for example a start-up bank loan, a foundation for start-ups or an angel investor.
- **Crowdfund:** use an online crowdfunding platform like Kickstarter to raise funds for your innovation.

There are many ways to succeed at innovation with no budget. However, there is another health warning, in that to develop organisational innovation you do need leadership and commitment. Without both commitment and leadership there is a risk that failed products are discarded and innovation is labelled as something that 'failed' and therefore not ever worth investing in.

Frugal innovation

Another innovation slogan has arrived! 'Frugal innovation' is more than just doing more with less. It focuses on creative ways to reuse what you already have and get more value from limited resources, to find better solutions that bring both business and social value. For example, in Lima, Peru, where there is high humidity and only about one inch of rainfall each year, an engineering college has created a huge advertising billboard that absorbs air humidity and converts it into purified water. This innovation, using limited and existing resources, produces 90 litres of clean water every day.

Frugal innovation, which originates from entrepreneurs in emerging markets, particularly India, is beginning to shift the corporate mindset for innovation in the West by focusing first on solving real problems without trying to create demand. Some big companies are focusing on 'radical affordability' and completely re-thinking designs to offer goods that sell for a small fraction of what traditional models cost, with an emphasis on simplicity to delight value-conscious customers.

 Watch Navi Radjou on TED for more on frugal innovation at:
www.ted.com/talks/navi_radjou_creative_problem_
solving_in_the_face_of_extreme_limits?language=en

Checklist

- Focus on the purpose and *choose* to innovate with no budget.
- Look for partners, for funding support, insight and idea delivery.
- Prioritise ruthlessly.
- Keep it simple and look to frugal innovation for inspiration.

Innovating when you feel like you are stuck

Do you want to innovate but you just don't know where to start? Or do you feel like you have been going round in circles on a project? Maybe you just have too many options and you can't decide which to go for?

We've all been there. Everyone gets stuck. It's part of life. We all have problems to solve, politics to overcome, too much choice, a tendency to procrastinate, slumps in motivation and focus. At one time or another in the innovation process it is inevitable that you will hit a wall.

There are several proven ways to push through being stuck and get moving again. First, look at yourself. Innovation is a tough job; you have to be physically and mentally strong to be resilient to the ups and downs that you will experience during an innovation process.

The five ways to mental wellbeing

The five ways to mental wellbeing were originally developed by the UK government as a way to tackle mental health and promote general wellbeing.[12] Apply them to help you work through the stuck times in innovation.

1. Connect . . . With the people around you. Building connections will support and enrich you every day.

[12]Government Office for Science, 2008. Mental capital and wellbeing. Available at: <https://www.gov.uk/government/uploads/system/uploads/attachment_data/file/292450/mental-capital-wellbeing-report.pdf>

2. Be active . . . Go for a walk or run. Step outside. Exercising makes you feel good. Find a physical activity you enjoy and that suits your level of mobility and fitness.

3. Take notice . . . Be curious. Savour the moment, whether you are walking to work, eating lunch or talking to friends. Be aware of the world around you.

4. Keep learning . . . Try something new. Learning new things will make you more confident as well as being fun.

5. Give . . . Do something nice for a friend, or a stranger. Thank someone. Smile. Feeling connected with the people around you can be rewarding.

Why are you stuck?

Ask yourself 'Why?' five times, as described on **page 7** to uncover the root cause of why you are stuck. Find a mentor to help you work through it. If you find yourself answering 'I don't know' try to break that pattern. Another question to ask yourself is, 'If I did know what made me stuck what would I say?'

- **It's part of the process:** being stuck is normal in innovation and it is part of the process of growth. Often, that 'stuck' feeling intensifies right before a breakthrough. Acknowledge that it is there for a reason, and work with it.

- **Reconnect** with your project's original purpose: Why is it important that you do this?

- **Reflection:** take a step back to reflect. Is this the right idea or project? Is this where you can best be focusing your efforts?

- **Acknowledge** how far you've come. If you have started a confidence diary as described on **page 138,** refer back to it. Give yourself a pep talk. You might not be as stuck as you think.

- **Eat a frog:** Mark Twain once said that if the first thing you do each morning is to eat a live frog, you can go through the day knowing that that is probably the worst thing that will happen to you all day. Your 'frog' is your biggest, most important task, the one you are most likely to procrastinate about. Select that important task that you have been putting off and make a start on it.

- **Break patterns** in your thinking and approach at the problem from a different perspective. You learned how to do this in **Step 5** by asking 'What if?' and 'How might we?'
- **Just start.** Stop thinking about what you have to do, and just do it. Force yourself to spend 15 minutes on anything to do with your innovation project.
- **Do nothing.** Take 10 minutes and change your perspective, go for a walk, call a friend, take a power nap. Do something that relaxes you and takes your mind off the problem.

What haven't I told you?

Sometimes in an innovation project where several people are working on discrete elements, it can be that individually you are stuck because you don't have all the information, but as a team you have the solution. There could be assumptions about what people know, or don't know, that inadvertently block solutions. There is a simple game called 'What haven't I told you?' that can help.

- The game is played in a round. You could invite the innovation project group as well as people with less direct knowledge because they will ask naïve questions that you miss when you are close to the project.
- One person is a facilitator and scribe.
- Everyone thinks of something that they know about the project and that they haven't heard anyone else talk about.
- If people are stuck (!) use the questions below to get them going.

If someone else were trying to sabotage my efforts, what information would they want to withhold from me, or change, or lie to me about?

Aside from my formal deliverables, what am I doing that anyone on the team could conceivably care about?

- For each round, everyone takes a turn telling their item to the group. The scribe records each item.
- After the ideas dry up, the group can identify new information that might help unstick them.

This game helps reduce the volume of knowledge that's held by each individual but hidden from the rest of the team, and it increases the volume of shared knowledge.

You don't need to be a team to benefit from playing this game. What haven't you told yourself?

Source: Brenner, R., 2002. What haven't I told you? Chaco Canyon Consulting. Available at: <http://www.chacocanyon.com/pointlookout/021211.shtml>

Checklist

- Accept that 'stuck' is part of the process.
- Look after yourself and build your personal wellbeing and resilience.
- Try a range of different tactics to break out of your 'stuckness'.

Part 3

10 common innovation challenges

Challenge 1   How do I develop my own innovation process or framework?

Challenge 2   How do I build an innovation network?

Challenge 3   How do I make time to innovate?

Challenge 4   How do I measure innovation?

Challenge 5   How do I motivate others to start to innovate?

Challenge 6   How do I create a culture of innovation?

Challenge 7   How do I manage failure?

Challenge 8   How do I innovate quickly?

Challenge 9   How do I approach a niche product?

Challenge 10 How do I recruit good innovators?

Whilst the approach to innovation can be different for every organisation, there are some common challenges that all innovators are likely to face. This part aims to address some of those common challenges and provide you with tactics to overcome them.

Challenge 1

How do I develop my own innovation process or framework?

Ultimately innovation has to be led from the top and as a long-term strategy it requires commitment. If you are not the leader, you can still choose the way you tackle innovation to drive change for your customers, yourself personally and your organisation.

An innovation process follows the steps in **Part 1** of this book supported by a culture that facilitates and allows innovation to flourish. It must be structured enough so people understand where to take their ideas, but flexible enough that it doesn't suck the energy and enthusiasm out of people because it has so many levels of sign-off.

Some considerations

There is no single right innovation process or framework. Take into consideration the following when developing yours.

- **Appetite:** what ambition is there for innovation? Why is innovation important?
- **Resources:** what resources do you have to support innovation: *Post-it Notes* and a sofa, or an investment budget?
- **Skills and experience:** do you have the skills and experience? Do you have good project managers skilled at driving new initiatives forward?
- **Capacity:** what capacity is there right now for innovation? Is there anything you can stop doing to allow time and space for innovation?

- **Current structure:** Is there a quick way to adapt current structures to include innovation? People resist change: the more aligned a new process is to existing ones, the fewer barriers there will be for implementation.

- **Simple:** make whatever process you decide on as simple as it can possibly be.

However you approach innovation keep it as simple as possible. Apply the basic principles in **Part 1**, summarised below, to *your* situation.

- **Pinpoint your purpose.** What is the purpose of your innovation? What is the big goal that you must achieve? The first part of the innovation process is, without sounding too over-dramatic, to define the purpose of it all.

- **Know and understand your customers.** It's more than just knowing what your customers buy, and their likes and dislikes, it's considering, *'if this is what I know then what does it mean?'* Find a way to make understanding customers and sharing that information part of everyone's role.

- **Decide your innovation focus.** Choose whether you will achieve your purpose through making incremental changes, developing new or better services or striving for disruption. Or you could go for a combination of all three.

- **Know your market now and in the future.** In addition to getting to grips with your customers' needs and wants, you must understand the marketplace that you are operating in, who your competition is and what market forces could impact on your innovation. Predicting and developing products that respond to trends in the future is an important skill because the environment is constantly changing.

- **Generate lots of ideas.** Generate ideas with your purpose and customers in mind. There are many ways to encourage ideas from employees, customers and wider networks: for example by running workshops, World Cafés, setting challenges or idea web platforms.

- **Filter and choose the best ideas.** You can involve employees as part of a workshop, or have a separate panel that decides which ideas to take forward. Being clear on your purpose and criteria helps you to make decisions about the ideas to progress and the ideas to stop.

- **Prototype, fail fast and refine.** A prototype is a sample or a model of your idea, whether it's a product, service or a new technology. Making a prototype brings your idea to life, helps you to refine it and gives opportunities to involve internal and external stakeholders.

- **Pilot, adapt and invest.** Piloting is testing your idea in a live environment on a small scale, for example with fewer participants, or a narrower geographical area. Piloting mitigates risks, helps you refine your plan, tests assumptions and gives an opportunity to test different variables. It can also help you convince sceptics that your idea could work as they can try the product or process without committing.

- **The business case.** This is needed to pitch for investment; it shows the detail including the market context, competitor activity, market segments, resources and expertise required to deliver, consideration of potential partners, as well as cost and income models and structures. The scale of the idea and investment required will dictate the level of sign-off required. A business case needs to be robust enough to make the case, but not so complex that it paralyses the development of the ideas. It also has to be a real part of the decision-making process and not a document that just because it exists, permits idea development.

- **Take your ideas to market.** Implement the business model and clear plans on how you will scale and sustain your innovation.

- **On-going feedback loop.** Once your idea is in the marketplace, that is just the start – you must constantly monitor its performance and adapt as customers and the environment change.

Your innovation process and framework will help ideas to develop and progress. However, a process and framework alone are not enough. For innovation to flourish you must also facilitate a culture that encourages and supports innovation. There is more on how to do this on **page 178.**

Checklist

- Organisational innovation must be led from the top, but you can still lead innovation in your own sphere of influence.
- Apply the basic framework principles to your situation and unique context.
- Make it as simple as possible.

Challenge 2

How do I build an innovation network?

Great innovators are connected. They have diverse networks across different sectors, countries and generations. They build their networks so they are there, ready to help on the day that they are needed.

Online networks

It is easy and cheap to build networks online, for example:

- **Twitter:** search for and follow people who tweet about the topics that you are interested in, retweet their posts, ask questions, spark conversations and add value by posting information or insights that will be of relevance to them.

- **Facebook:** whether you use it for personal connections or your organisation's page, add value by commenting, posting or liking.

- **LinkedIn:** for professional networks, be rigorous in extending your virtual address book by Linking-in to everyone you meet. Use the search options to find people you would like to connect with, or ask your current connections to make introductions. If you are making an approach to someone you do not know, don't send the standard automated invite to connect. Personalise it with a line about who you are and why you would like to connect.

In real life

Online provides vast opportunities for you to develop meaningful relationships that you can strengthen in real life. Face-to-face conversations that flow, spark and develop ideas give a greater degree of trust and understanding of each other.

Actively seek the places where different networks intersect that will open up new opportunities. Going to events that everyone goes to is a cop-out – it's just a social. Seek events that are outside your usual industry. Next time a colleague invites you to something leftfield, or when that interesting but random email invite for a list that you don't recall signing up to arrives – go to it.

Many people can find meeting new people uncomfortable and dread the thought of networking. If that is you then here are some tips to make your networking more tolerable and perhaps even enjoyable.

- **Change your mindset:** stop using the word *networking*. What you are doing is sharing your expertise and ideas and adding value to others.

- **Who:** what are your goals? Who would you like to meet, either specific names, or types of people, e.g. CEO of a tech start-up, someone who is your target customer, a potential funder? Do your research and be focused about who you want to meet.

- **What do you want?** In most circumstances the outcome of a 'networking' conversation is an invitation to have a coffee and a longer chat on another day. Don't put yourself under pressure to nail the innovation agenda on your first meeting.

- **You:** focus on what you can give. What value can you add to the people you meet?

- **Agile:** don't get stuck with one person. A neat way to move through the room is to ask who you can introduce the other person to.

- **Tactics:** approach open groups, rather than two people in deep conversation. Open groups are easier to join which will in turn boost your confidence.

Ask for what you want and give back in return

If you want help with your innovation, your network is there to help you in the same way as you are there for them. Simply ask for what you want. I often use Twitter to get introductions to people I would like to ask for help or advice, for example I post 'I would like a connection to the Finance Director at xyz company' or 'Do you know a health-conscious mum who has a baby under one year of age?' I also help people when they make similar requests of me.

Building rapport (making people like you)

People like people who are like them. People want to work with people they like and get on with.

When we communicate we do so through our tone of voice, body language and the words we use. Your body language, tone of voice and what you say adds up to a person making an opinion of you and in this case whether they choose to collaborate, help you or even fund your innovation. Here are three tactics to help you.

- **Matching and mirroring.** Start to notice your words and body language more. You can build rapport with people by matching and mirroring their body language, words and tone. You do this naturally already, but become more aware of it and subtly refine your skills.

- **Active listening.** How often do you do more than one thing at a time and partially concentrate on both? How many times does someone speak to you and you don't properly listen? How does it feel to not be listened to or paid attention to? By changing your behaviour, show you are listening by leaning in, making eye contact and gestures like nods to demonstrate your undivided attention, and quickly build rapport.

- **Yes and. . . .** Have you ever had an idea that you suggested be killed outright? How did it feel? It's easy to kill ideas because you know they haven't worked before, or that it's unlikely to get budget. One simple shift in language from 'no but' (that won't work) to 'yes and' (help me understand how that can work this time) makes a big impact on others. Start to notice when you use the negative 'no but' and change it to 'yes and'. It doesn't mean you agree with everything, but it signals your positive approach to building on an idea.

Checklist

- Build your networks before you need them, both on and offline.
- Meet people in real life at events outside your 'normal' network.
- Listen and build on ideas to gain rapport.
- Ask for help and think about how you add value and help others in return.

How do I make time to innovate?

Even if your chief executive puts innovation as one of the organisation's priorities, finding time for innovation projects can be a challenge as more immediate and important priorities take over, and constant interruptions mean that it's easy to deprioritise innovation time.

While ideas are valuable, the input that really matters is time: if you don't make time your ideas won't happen. You don't have time *not* to innovate, so you have to find a way.

To do this requires a shift in mindset. Innovation is not something you do after you get your work done. It's *how* you approach your work. Unstructured time alone isn't enough to spur innovation; it has to be part of a broader innovation process and culture which when done right, can lead to breakthrough ideas and products.

Google is infamous for its 20 per cent time, allowing employees the equivalent of a day a week to innovate on their own ideas, which has produced several successful Google products, including Gmail. We can't all be Google so we have to take the principle of prioritising time to innovate in a way that is realistic and workable for us.

And it is a challenge. Innovation is a discipline, just as working out is a discipline for an athlete. That's why it's essential to balance the tactical activities with strategic activities and set some boundaries. If you're not disciplined and committed to making time, then you are just paying lip service to innovation.

Here are some ways to make time for innovation:

- **Chunks.** Some periods of time are littered with project deadlines and the day, half day, hour or whatever time you allocated for regular innovation gets squeezed. A way to overcome this is to accumulate your time into chunks. Five hours a week is 20 hours a month, so schedule chunks of innovation time after all those deadlines. This works at Intuit, a US software company, which encourages its people to take bigger chunks of time for innovation, like an innovation mini break. It allows for scheduling and planning of innovation around deadlines and workloads and makes innovation time more likely to happen.

- **People.** Innovation time can be spent with other people to spark and develop ideas with. Gather a team of people to take the time with you. It could be your actual team, or a more diverse mix of people from within and outside the organisation. Don't make the assumption that this time put aside for innovation has to be alone time if that's not how you work best. Involving cross-divisional groups also helps to work innovation into the organisational culture.

- **Focus.** Structure your innovation time to help you focus, for example you could join or run an innovation lock-in to work continuously for one or two days to move an idea forward. They can be fun too (especially if you like pizza).

Practical tips to make time for innovation

- Get senior management buy-in. Whatever your proposal, if making time is going to work it has to be championed from the top.
- Decide on how much time is practical for your situation, but still enough that allows dedicated time to achieve something.
- Make participation voluntary. Not everyone will want to be involved. That's OK.
- Invite people from across the whole organisation, and consider people from outside, for example entrepreneurs and customers.

- Apply some structure to help people focus on the broad areas they are innovating about.
- Review progress, for example in one-to-one meetings, so people are accountable.
- Support and communicate, for example through online tools like wikis, or physical meeting space like access to the conference room or a budget for off-site space.
- Record and share ideas, both successes and also shelved ideas that someone might want to come back to at a later date. (Like with *Post-its*!)
- Consider rewards and incentives, for example bonuses or extra holiday days . For some, simply being given the trust and freedom to work on your own exciting idea can be incentive enough.
- Manage expectations as innovation may not deliver immediate results; you have to give time to giving time.
- Develop and refine this process, based on feedback, and view it as a pilot in itself.

Case study

GeoVation

Ordnance Survey, Great Britain's national mapping agency, makes time for innovation through its GeoVation challenge programme. Driven by consumer feedback to make data more accessible and address specific community needs which may be satisfied, in part, through the use of geography, the GeoVation challenge begins with a challenging question that participants, including staff, entrepreneurs, developers, community groups and innovators, attempt to solve.

A panel selects the successful entrants who get to spend two days in a supportive environment – a GeoVation camp – where together with subject matter experts, developers and user groups entrants build ideas and develop them into fundable, sustainable business offerings.

Working from the premise that innovation = problem ×
solution/s × execution, Geovation places a big emphasis on
funding the winning ideas and supporting their execution.

Over the last 5 years GeoVation challenges have involved
over 2,650 people, generated 670 ideas, invited 86 teams
to develop their ideas into prototype ventures at GeoVation
camp, and funded 31 challenge projects which have been
launched or are in development.

GeoVation camps themselves have been a pilot to test
whether an open approach to innovation can deliver results.
With tangible results and a community committed to
developing sustainable workable ideas, GeoVation is now
being developed as an internal mechanism at Ordnance Survey
to drive both a culture and process for effective innovation.

Checklist

- Get senior-level buy-in.
- Find a way to make time that is workable for *you*.
- Chunks of time can have more benefits than regular weekly
  time slots.

Challenge 4

How do I measure innovation?

According to McKinsey, more than 70 per cent of corporate leaders claim that innovation is in their top three business priorities, yet only 22 per cent set innovation measures.[13] The nebulous nature of innovation makes it difficult to measure. However, without meaningful metrics you cannot know if you are successful in achieving your innovation goals or how to improve your innovation performance.

The other extreme is when organisations measure absolutely everything they can think of around their innovation programme and their employees become a slave to the metrics, not the innovation. This level of measurement sucks the passion and enthusiasm out of people, and innovation grinds to a halt.

Defining the right metrics for your organisation can be tricky. There's generally no one right answer. It takes a combination of art and science, to balance measuring simple and meaningful metrics that give the information needed, yet still keep people inspired to achieve their goals. In addition, every organisation has its own culture, and therefore must fine-tune what it measures to reinforce the goals, values and norms that it requires for inspiring its innovation.

[13]Barsh, J. et al., 2008. Leadership and innovation. McKinsey & Company. Available at: <http://www.mckinsey.com/insights/innovation/leadership_and_innovation>

Setting your innovation measures

1. The first step is to be absolutely clear on the strategic objective of your innovation programme. Is it to grow the business, reposition to a new marketplace, develop a better working culture or create new value for customers? What does success look like?

2. With a clear strategic objective you can then define the innovation goals that support that objective. For example, is it to increase revenue by 50 per cent in the next five years, be market leader in a different category in three years, reduce costs through staff attrition by 30 per cent in the next financial year, increase income by 15 per cent from incremental product development or disrupt the market?

3. Next identify the innovation capabilities – the people measures required for the future. What does the culture for innovation look like, how do managers and teams need to behave to implement innovation across all areas?

4. Agree both input and output measures that support both the overall innovation strategy and people as well as individual business or idea areas.

Input measures

Input measures are what you invest in innovation and include financial investment as well as training or time on innovation projects. Some examples of the types of inputs you could choose to measure are:

- Percentage of capital invested in innovation activities.

- Percentage of 'outside' vs 'inside' inputs to the innovation process (open innovation). For example, Procter & Gamble uses an input metric focused on 'the percentage of external sourcing of ideas and technology' as a way to drive its Connect and Develop strategy for open innovation. In 2000, 10 per cent of the company's R&D was outsourced – today, 50 per cent of all ideas and technology come from the outside.

- Percentage of employees who have received training and tools for innovation e.g. analysing insight, idea generation, or facilitation techniques.

- Existence of formal structures and processes that support innovation.
- Number of new competencies (distinctive skills and knowledge that drive innovation).
- Percentage of executives' time spent on strategic innovation versus day-to-day operations.
- Percentage of managers with training in the concepts and tools of innovation.
- Percentage of product/service or strategic innovation projects with assigned executive sponsors.

Output measures

Measuring outputs is another balancing act; make them too broad and your measuring becomes unwieldy and hard to manage, but make them too prescriptive and you can stifle creativity.

3M churns out around 400 new products and 500 new patents each year. It achieves this diversity by having innovation outcomes that are not too specific. For example, to generate 35 per cent of sales from products that are less than four years old, and 10 per cent of sales from products that have only been around for one year. This sets a high target for the pace of innovation.

Output measures that you could consider are:

- number of new products, services, launched in current or new markets in the past year/X years;
- percentage of revenue/profit from products or services introduced in the past year/X years;
- royalty and licensing income from patents/intellectual property;
- number of innovations delivered/in the pipeline that significantly advance existing businesses versus small tweaks to existing products or services;
- number of new ideas implemented/not implemented;
- speed to market/speed of innovation project completion (should increase year on year);
- number of and what lessons learned from failures (and successes);

- number of existing customers that trade up to next-generation products or services;
- number of new innovations that come from external sources like crowdsourcing or open innovation;
- increased number of new ideas/improved quality of ideas;
- impact on brand and image indicated through brand image surveys, customer feedback, and analyst rankings;
- engagement of employees, external partners, customers, suppliers (e.g. number of ideas submitted/people involved in the process);
- number and percentage of projects that are in the innovation pipeline that are judged to be high quality.

Measures are not an end in themselves. Build learning loops from both successes and failures into the process and revisit measures on an on-going basis as your innovation capabilities, projects and programme develops and improves over time.

Checklist for measuring innovation

- Measure innovation based on the big thinking innovation goals that you set out to achieve.
- Only measure what is important – don't kill innovation by measuring everything.
- Consider appropriate input and output measures.
- Evaluate the process and adapt as required.

How do I motivate others to start to innovate?

Giving people the opportunity and freedom to collaborate with others to learn new skills and be rewarded for delivering meaningful work is motivating. Innovation and motivation are intrinsically linked. If you get your innovation programme right, it will be motivating for everyone involved.

The biggest challenge is motivating people to start. Many people either don't perceive themselves as creative or innovative, or haven't been given the opportunity or encouragement, or simply don't know where to begin.

Believing we can be creative is the first step. Then we have to let go of preconceptions and processes that exist in a corporate environment and open ourselves up to new thinking. We have to unlearn how to think in order to relearn how to think. This can be really liberating but can feel uncomfortable and unnerving all at the same time.

Free word association

One tactic that helps you let go of preconceptions is free word association. So let's practise. But before you start, paradoxically, there are a few rules for this exercise:

- Don't censor or analyse your ideas as you are doing the exercise. Just write them down.
- Aim not to have any repeated words in your list.
- There must be an association or connection for *you* between the word you write down and the previous word on the list. What do you immediately think of when you read the word? Capture the first thought that comes to your mind.

Now you are ready to start

1. Pick up a book or magazine that is to hand. Randomly open it on any page. Close your eyes and place your finger on the page. Use the word your finger is pointing at as the first word for this exercise.

2. Write the word down on a piece of paper.

3. Underneath it, write down the first word that you associate with the word.

4. Underneath that word, write down a word that you associate with the second word, and so on.

5. Keep adding words to the list for three minutes, and work as quickly as you can. You should aim to write a list of at least 25 words in the three minutes. The technique of putting yourself under the pressure of achieving a goal within a certain time limit helps to stop your analysing too.

You have to practise letting go of your preconceptions. Practise free word association every day if you can. You can also do this exercise verbally in pairs or groups taking it in turns to free word associate.

This is a technique used by improvisers. A skill of improvisation is letting go and using free association to build ideas.

 You can learn and practise more at:
www.youtube.com/user/hooplaimprov

Start with something meaningful

A simple way to motivate people to innovate is to get them working on something that is meaningful to them. Get a group together that you need to motivate to innovate.

Set some rules:

- All ideas are valid.
- As many ideas as possible are required.
- Be candid – don't hold back.

Pose the question: 'If you could kill or change all the stupid rules that get in the way of better serving our customers or just doing your job, what would they be and how would you do it?'

- Ask people to discuss and write down all their ideas.
- Give them as much time as you can/they need – whatever happens first.
- Ask everyone to write their 'favourite' stupid rule on a *Post-it Note.*
- Then have each place his or her rule on a whiteboard grid that has two axes: Y is ease of implementation, and X is degree of impact.

	Hard to implement with low impact	Hard to implement with high impact
Y = Ease of implementation	Easy to implement with low impact	Easy to implement with high impact

X = Degree of impact

- Discuss the results.
- Some of the same rules will show up multiple times. Some will be rules only one person follows. Some won't be formal rules, falling more into the 'But that's how we've always done things' category.
- And some won't be rules at all: meetings just for the sake of meeting, reports that no one reads, multiple sign-offs for purchases or approvals. . . .
- Let the group pick a few easy to implement/high impact rules – and kill those rules on the spot.
- Make a ceremony, go on, set fire to the notes and dance on the embers.

- Some rules you can't kill on the spot. A few might first require changes in process or workflow.
- Make the necessary changes to the rules immediately where you can.
- Let everyone know when those rules are killed.

Employees who report that their opinion and ideas matter to their employer also confirm higher levels of engagement and satisfaction at work. An action focused 'can do' approach sparks imagination and creativity as well as motivating people when they know that their input was listened to and acted upon.

Source: Bodell, L. (2013). Want to spark innovation? Try killing stupid rules. [online] Available at: <http://www.dukece.com/elements/docs/Bodell-Innovation.pdf>

Case study

easyJet

The airline easyJet inspired innovation by bringing teams together that work on the ground. Together they took time to understand the problems that they unknowingly caused each other and came up with a range of solutions. These solutions made working together better and made improvements for business, claiming to have reduced plane turnaround time from 40 to 25 minutes.

Source: Kingdon, M., (2012). *The science of serendipity*. John Wiley & Sons: Chichester.

Checklist

- Work on challenging preconceptions with free word association every day.
- Motivate people by working on something important to them.
- Build trust and motivation by taking action.

How do I create a culture of innovation?

You can have the best innovation process in the world, but without a culture or an environment that supports it, innovation will fail. Organisations that are successful at innovation have a clear process *and* foster the right climate for their employees to innovate.

How you create a culture where innovation can thrive will depend on what your current culture is and what you want to achieve through innovation. For example, one of Facebook's innovation principles is 'Move fast and break things'. This works for Facebook, a young start-up, but might not work for organisations that have historical baggage for risk aversion, such as your local NHS Trust or a china shop.

Below are 10 principles that are the starting blocks from which you can build *your* innovation culture in your team or organisation.

1. **Leadership:** in order for the entire organisation to have innovation flowing through its DNA, it has to be visibly led by the chief executive and senior teams. You can however, lead in your team or area of influence.

2. **The big picture purpose:** articulate simply the fundamental reason why it is important to commit to innovation. What is the statement that inspires and focuses people? For example, every employee at Pixar is responsible for enriching people's lives through stories, and the teams at CRUK are working so that together they will beat cancer. And of course at NASA, according to the story of when President Kennedy made an unexpected visit in the 1960s and asked the man sweeping

the floor what his job was: the man replied, 'Helping to put a man on the moon.'

3. **Tell everyone:** invest resource to ensure that everyone in your organisation understands innovation and knows what it means to them, specifically in their day-to-day work. Communication is vital throughout the whole innovation process. For example, Four Seasons CEO Katie Taylor worked with senior leaders to develop an innovation handbook and videos for the organisation's 35,000 employees.

4. **Time to innovate:** make getting away from the day-to-day tasks to focus on other projects normal. It might be time to incubate ideas or to work on projects that are out of scope or with other teams or follow passions, interests and hunches. For example, 3M gives 15 per cent time, which gave Art Fry time to look at shelved products that eventually led him to *Post-it Note* fame.

5. **Incentives:** find a way to motivate people to want to be involved in innovation – some organisations have cash based incentive schemes, others offer additional holiday days. For some employees the opportunity to be involved in the development of their idea is incentive enough.

6. **Allow failure:** innovation is new, and whilst a good process of prototyping, piloting and testing will manage risk, your idea is never guaranteed to work. Some ideas will fail. Encourage colleagues to take managed risks and then get together to talk about their failures, share them, learn from them and move on. See **Step 8** for more on failure.

7. **Don't dabble:** Yoda said, '*Do or not do, there is no try.*' This applies to innovation. If you choose to commit to innovation you have to allocate adequate effort, time and resource. Dabbling in innovation, saying you are committed but not following through with action, demotivates teams and breaks trust, and you become part of the movement that has turned innovation into a no substance buzzword. Innovation is a long-term business strategy, and is unlikely to deliver results overnight, so you have to be absolutely committed to seeing it through.

8. **Connect people:** consider the physical environment that you work in every day. Create water cooler opportunities where people in an email-centric virtual world have real face-to-face

conversations. When Steve Jobs was at Pixar, he put the mailboxes, meeting rooms, cafeteria and bathrooms at the centre of the offices to increase the opportunities for people to have conversations.

9. **Get everyone involved:** make sure that everyone has an opportunity to add value wherever they are based and whatever their role. For example, Four Seasons gives every employee, and especially those who are closest to its customers, from bartenders to cooks, concierge to reception staff, the power to suggest and implement new ideas.

10. **Just do it:** that old forgiveness over permission cliché is for you. You won't change a culture overnight. It takes time. Starting is often the hardest part. Just do it.

Case study

Innocent

Innocent leapt to fame in 1999 when three friends asked their customers at a music festival whether they should quit their day jobs and make smoothies. Their customers said just do it – so they did. One of Innocent's strategies was to drive business growth through a culture of innovation. They allocate seating randomly, including management, so people get to know and understand different functions. They have communal kitchen space and employees are encouraged to hang out there, have meetings, eat cake and fill up with smoothies. The office design has multiple social spaces that encourage informal meetings: water cooler moments. There is a social atmosphere and all sorts of activities from knitting to karate are encouraged. There is something important about building ideas together, but also an acknowledgement that innovation can be tricky and you have more chance of working through problems and differences if you have eaten cake and drunk tea together.

Innocent never underestimates the power of human connection in helping have ideas and moving them forward quickly. The company encourages its staff to suggest ways to improve the business, for example veg pots (now discontinued) were a result of an internal brief for the 'next big thing' for Innocent which was worth £30 million at retail, and Juicy Water was an underperforming product that a staff member suggested was rebranded, after which profits more than doubled.

Sources: Engage for Success, 2013. Case study: employee innovation at Innocent. *Engage for Success* [online]. Available at <http://www. engageforsuccess.org/ideas-tools/case-study-employee-innovation-at-innocent/#.VWM-9Ye4kdU> Groves, K., 2011.

How Innocent Drinks has kept their youthful workplace spirit despite growth. *enviableworkplace.com* [online] Available at: <http://enviableworkplace.com/growing-up-but-staying-innocent/>

Inside Fruit Towers, the Innocent office

Checklist

- Understand your current culture and environment.
- Lead by example, wherever you work in your organisation.
- Communicate and involve everyone, facilitate relationship building.
- Consider how the physical working space can encourage innovation.

How do I manage failure?

'If you are not failing every now and then you are not doing anything very innovative.'

Woody Allen, actor and comedian

If you are taking innovation seriously, if you are pushing to drive change either incrementally, radically or through the development of new products and services, it is inevitable that there will be some failures along the way. No human being can possibly foresee all the consequences of an innovation, no matter how obvious they may seem in hindsight.

Because failure feels uncomfortable we tend to gloss over it. Either we don't admit to the failure, or brush it under the carpet as quickly as possible, or we even change the measures so that it doesn't appear to be quite the failure that it actually was. The important detail is learning from failure so that we don't make the same mistakes again, wasting unnecessary time and resource. Successful innovators have a brave attitude to failure and create a supportive environment in which sharing failure is an accepted part of the culture.

Following the steps in this book of prototyping, piloting and adapting your ideas will help you minimise the risk of failure but any new innovation comes with uncertainty; long-term benefits are not always clear and certainly never guaranteed at the time that you develop ideas. So accept that it is inevitable that some ideas will fail and prepare for it. Here are some suggestions:

- Hold a pre-mortem: consider all the things that could go wrong with a project at the start and then ensure there is something in the plan to mitigate against that happening.

- Asking the question, 'What's the worst that can happen?' helps you to build contingency plan. Preparing for the very worst can help to really confront failure and often helps us realise that the worst-case scenario is in fact manageable.

- Reframe failure as a test: the purpose of a test is to establish if something will work or not. In simple terms there are two answers, yes it worked or no it didn't. So even if your pilot didn't work, it wasn't a failure because the point was to test if it worked or not. Reframing failure as a test can help make it easier to discuss.

- Have failure as an item in a team meeting; include discussion about projects that were 'tested' and the results. Regularly talking about things that didn't work helps to make the topic of failure less uncomfortable.

- Fail yea! An events team reframed failure as acceptable by calling the agenda item on the team meeting 'fail yea!'. In this item, the team evaluated their events; they were really robust in unpicking both the parts of the event that went well and parts that could be done better. For example, they reached the attendance target, but what activity could they do differently to attract more attendees next time? The result was a steady growth in their events income.

- Make regular debriefs at each stage of every project to check progress as well as an evaluation at the end of a project. Be really rigorous about celebrating the things that worked well as well as things that didn't and spend time working on how you could do *both* better.

- Reward: consider how you can reward failure to make it acceptable. For example, Greenpeace had an infamous *Dog's Bollocks Award*, that was an honour to be nominated for because for an independent organisation campaigning for a sustainable world, if no one was taking some risks, really pushing to test new ways to drive change, then they were not doing the very best job they could.

- Share learning: is there a place to share failure, an intranet, internal newsletter or a wall of failure where all staff post the things that fail on a regular basis?

- Call failure something different, for example Four Seasons stopped labelling something a failure or a mistake, and instead called it a glitch. The rationale is that a failure or a mistake is final, something you can't take back, but a glitch is an opportunity to recover and build a relationship in the process.

 Check out the museum of failed products for failure inspiration at:

http://courses.ischool.berkeley.edu/i202/f12/node/296

Case study

New Coke

In 1985, in response to its declining market share and the increasing popularity of its key rival Pepsi, Coca-Cola launched *New Coke*.

At the time, Pepsi's advertising campaigns were based around asking the public if they could taste the difference between *Pepsi* and *Coke*. They could – and they preferred the taste of *Pepsi*.

In response, Coca-Cola developed a new sweeter tasting formula. After conducting over 200,000 taste tests, which according to the taste testers not only tasted better than the old *Coke*, but also tasted better than *Pepsi*, *New Coke* was ready for launch.

However, on 23 April 1985 when *New Coke* was launched and old *Coke* was taken out of circulation, it was a disaster. Customers were horrified that their *Coke* had been changed. On 11 July 1985, Coca-Cola withdrew *New Coke* and reinstated old *Coke*.

So what happened?

'We did not understand the deep emotions of so many of our customers for Coca-Cola,' said company President Donald R. Keough.

The development of *New Coke* was all about taste and overlooked the importance of the relationship customers had with the brand. Until the launch of *New Coke*, Coca-Cola's brand had been about its 'original' status. For example, in

1942 magazine adverts in the US: 'The only thing like Coca-Cola is Coca-Cola itself. It's the real thing.' If you tell the world you have the 'real thing' you cannot then just come up with a 'new real thing'. To make matters worse, since 1982 *Coke*'s strapline had been 'Coke is it'. Now it was telling customers that actually *Coke* wasn't it, but *New Coke* was now it instead. Coca-Cola was fighting a taste battle with Pepsi in response to Pepsi's marketing campaign. What Coca-Cola overlooked was that the battle was not about taste, and it underestimated the value of brand loyalty and the heritage of Coca-Cola. Ironically, through the brand failure of *New Coke*, loyalty to 'the real thing' intensified and Coke recovered its market position with old *Coke*, repositioned as *Coke Classic*.

Some conspiracy theorists say the whole campaign had been planned in order to reaffirm public loyalty for Coca-Cola. But whether it was planned or not, the failure of *New Coke* affirmed the value of the brand and with that insight *Coke Classic* went on to retake the leading market position.

Learning important insights from its failure was key to Coca-Cola's reclaimed success over Pepsi.

Source: Marketing 91, 2015. Coca Cola brand failure. *Marketing 91*, [online]. Available at: <http://www.marketing91.com/coca-cola-brand-failure/>

Checklist

- Create an environment that makes it acceptable to fail.
- Really consider the worst that can happen – and plan for it.
- Facilitate talking openly about failure.
- Ensure that you understand why something failed and share it.

How do I innovate quickly?

A typical product development cycle from initial idea to market can take over two years. This also means that the ideas in development must still be relevant in two years' time. The longer your idea to market cycle is, the more disruptive your ideas need to be to be relevant in that future space, which paradoxically can further slow you down.

Often big organisations, even with the best innovation process, can be frustratingly slow. Working through a process, engaging the right teams, evaluating ideas, seeking collaboration, permissions and sign-off all takes time. Both innovation and speed can be compromised by too much bureaucracy and control.

Small businesses are often able to innovate more quickly than big ones, however they can still become stuck. Whatever the size of your business follow the principles below to innovate quickly:

- **Think big.** Connect back to your purpose and focus on why you must innovate quickly. Maybe it's an immediate threat, a competitor has just launched a product that is going to wipe your company out of existence, or maybe it is because you have found a burning platform that has identified vulnerabilities that must be worked on, or maybe your strategy is to disrupt the marketplace and you just want to do it *now*.

- **Go small.** Learn from fast-moving entrepreneur start-ups and create a small focused team (often referred to as skunkworks) charged with driving innovation quickly that works outside of the constraints of the core business. For example, in the 1980s General Motors ran a project to launch a new line of vehicles that was detached from the parent company. It was to compete with Japanese vehicles (and more recently, EDF, which purchased shares in young companies) to bring creativity and knowledge of new markets to the group.

Some things to consider if you choose to set up a skunkworks to innovate quickly are as follows:

- The size of the group is small. Amazon founder and CEO Jeff Bezos has a rule that the team has to be small enough to be easily fed by two pizzas.
- The team involves the subject-matter experts who are required to deliver the project as well as outsiders with start-up experience who can challenge assumptions and bring a genuine small start-up mindset to the team.
- There is also a criterion of openness and collaboration for team members. In his 'design thinking' approach, Tim Brown, the IDEO boss, refers to the 'T-shaped people'; the vertical part of the T stands for speciality and the horizontal part for openness.
- One person leads this team who is responsible for making quick decisions and who understands the project in its entirety.
- Everyone has well-defined roles and responsibilities.
- Decision-making power is defined by a set of boundary conditions of schedule, cost and performance, meaning there is no need for reporting back, provided that the project remains within these boundaries.
- Central management delegates authority to the team and gives them permission to just do it.

Learn fast

This small team must learn fast. They do not spend time over-analysing, or creating business plans and spreadsheets. They spend time understanding their offering in the market, exploring key questions such as whether the technology will work, whether the product concept will meet customer needs, and whether customers will prefer it over the competitive alternatives. They prototype and test, learn, adapt and repeat. These are the lean start-up principles that we learned in **Step 2:** that it is better to fail many small times than one big time. Eric Ries says: 'Everything a start-up does is understood to be an experiment designed to achieve validated learning.' The faster you learn what doesn't work, the more time you can spend on what does. This approach enables you to change your strategy but without changing your big idea.

Case study

Learning fast and taking an idea to market

Carlsberg's largest cider brand, *Somersby*, was taken from initial concept to launch in Switzerland in under six months.

Using a new hybrid of crowdsourcing and word-of-mouth marketing Carlsberg created a successful launch in a difficult market, helping the brand to achieve awareness of 6 per cent before it even launched and reach 20 per cent of the Swiss population (1.5 million people) by launch, without any 'traditional' media activity.

Switzerland is not an easy place to launch an international cider drink; the market share of imported cider is just 2 per cent.

Carlsberg wanted to get a product to market fast. The team needed more insight on Swiss consumers and their views on cider but also needed to understand how to generate awareness.

The project kicked off in December 2013 with a planned launch in April 2014, meaning results had to be delivered under considerable time pressure. Carlsberg used a 'Consumer Co-creation Crowd' in which a community of people were recruited to a platform and were asked to generate insights, then ideas and then actively participate in the brand's launch as ambassadors for *Somersby*. This participation included trying the drink, hosting parties and using social media to promote the brand.

This approach, delivered quickly by the brand management team, allowed research, validation and word-of-mouth marketing to happen simultaneously and at a fraction of the cost of the traditional process, and dramatically faster than the 'usual' approach.

Checklist

- Think big, be clear on why innovating quickly is important.
- Form a discrete team that has a mandate to go fast outside of innovation as usual (IAU).
- Apply lean startup principles.

How do I approach a niche product?

A niche product is a simple, specialised product or service. It focuses on the needs of customers in a narrowly defined market, for example, dog owners, creative female freelancers, ceramic collectors, elderly fishing enthusiasts or brides to be.

Examples of narrowly defined markets, customers and products are:

- organic food – a narrowly defined part of the overall food market for customers concerned about the environment and/or seeking better quality;
- shampoo for swimmers – a narrowly defined part of the shampoo market for customers who swim regularly and want good conditioned hair;
- specialist cycling clothing sizes – a narrowly defined part of the sports clothing market, for customers who don't fit into usual skinny cycling clothes, like the UK company 'Fat Lad at the back.'

 http://fatladattheback.com

How do I develop a niche product?

The success of niche products, like all innovation, absolutely relies on knowing your customers, as well as the ability to develop and market your product in a way that resonates with them.

Being different is key. The more specific you can be in your research and offerings, the greater chance you have of developing something different and the greater the likelihood of niche success. Whether you yearn to be the go to place for toothbrushes for customers with toddlers, or the premier producer of cheese-less pizzas for pizza lovers with cheese allergies, when deciding on your niche you need to work through the following steps.

- **Are you ready?** Before you decide to go niche consider whether you have, or how you obtain, the competencies and capabilities to deliver a niche product to a niche market.
- **What is your focus?** What is the purpose of your innovation, your goal? What are you setting out to achieve?
- **Know your customer.** Succeeding in a niche market means you're starting with a limited number of buyers, so you need to get to know them intimately. Refer to **Step 2** for tactics to get to know your customer.
- **Identify customers' unique needs.** Look for ways to tailor your product or service to meet your customer's unique needs; consider how you can adapt, add to, combine, personalise, imitate, simplify or make your offering better. Assess the potential for additional related niche products: for example, if people have phones they may need covers too.
- **Be an expert.** Connect with your niche marketplace's key decision makers, enthusiasts and influencers by using social networks to learn to speak their language. Place yourself as an expert, as one of them.
- **Reach your customers.** Join or create online groups, feeds and networks that are relevant to your simple service. Optimise your landing page and blog. What tradeshows, conferences and meetings can you attend to reach your audience?
- **Develop marketing.** The marketing of your product could be the difference between success and failure. Consider how you can set your niche product apart from the rest of your offering as well as from your competitors. Develop packaging and messaging to make the product stand out.
- **Pricing.** The more tightly you define your prospects the more you can distinguish your offering, enabling you to charge a premium.
- **Test and adapt.** Continuously test to ensure your product and message are resonating with your target market.
- **Results.** Match your results back to your goals.

What if my niche is a fad or it has no shelf life?

Your initial product offer has potential to change and evolve significantly over time based on customer feedback. You can ask your customers to help you design new services or products (see open innovation **page 131**). Working closely with your customers gives many development opportunities.

You can offer additional services or products based on the actual needs of your customers. For example, a dog grooming parlour might also expand to doggy teeth cleaning. Tools to help children concentrate at school could also be developed for adults in the workplace.

Benefits to niche

- Develops a loyal customer base.
- Highly defined markets are often over-looked, under-served or disenfranchised by larger competitors , which means there is likely to be less competition.
- Niche marketing can be extremely cost-effective when you know exactly who your audience is and can be very, very specific. For example, it's cheaper to advertise in the *Angling Times* whose readers are your niche audience than in *The Sunday Times* or a broader audience.
- Focusing on a niche allows companies to focus on meeting the needs of a smaller group of customers without compromising their chance to increase the appeal to a broader market. For example, Hewlett-Packard markets all-in-one machines that print and scan to home office markets, and also targets larger businesses for separate, higher spec, printers and scanners.

Case study

Thomas Cook (India) Ltd

This company operates in a competitive global market, and has turned to a niche strategy to grow its travel business.

The company identified different niche segments and focused on developing products for each. It gave quirky, and sometimes funny, names for its niche itineraries to catch the imagination of its customers. For example:

Rock-On Holidays, for young, free, independent travellers feature engaging and experiential itineraries, including stays in party capitals of the world, snorkelling and glacier and alpine treks.

Travel & Learn, for the youth market, particularly school/university students, feature learning experiences, like visits to NASA, space simulation programmes, and interviews with rocket scientists, students and faculties in universities abroad, as well as activities like visits to theme parks, special classes for dance, music, painting and scuba diving.

Source: Krishna Kumar, P., 2013. Thomas Cook India: Forging ahead with production innovation & niche segments. Available at: <http://www.travelbizmonitor.com/Business-Strategy/thomas-cook-india-forging-ahead-with-product-innovation-niche-segments-20656>

Checklist

- Understand and stay in touch with your customers.
- Position yourself/your organisation *as* one of your expert customers.
- Focus on serving those customer needs as they develop.

How do I recruit good innovators?

People make change happen, which makes innovation primarily about people. Your success hinges on the people you work with to deliver your innovation. Invest time to get the right mix of attitude, skills and experience from the beginning.

Innovation team or everyone's role?

Whether to put a specific team in charge of innovation or make innovation part of every employee's role will depend on purpose, current culture and structure, skills, experience and resource. Generally, if you give the task of innovation to a team it signals that they are the only team that do innovation and that it is not part of other people's everyday role. The innovation team can become a dumping ground for ideas that people don't want to, or don't know how to develop, or can be perceived as the team that takes away the good and exciting projects. Either way, if not carefully managed and communicated, an innovation team can unintentionally turn into a skunkworks siloed department.

In a series of interviews conducted with senior leaders and innovation managers (predominantly in NGOs) for a nfpSynergy 'Innovation (still) Rules!' report in 2012, the interviewees felt that innovation should be part of everyone's role and not be tasked to a separate team. Some organisations advocated having an innovation team for a set period of time to kick-start a culture or process, or innovate quickly, which then reverted into business as usual once it was established.

You can download Innovation (still) Rules for free here:
http://nfpsynergy.net/innovation-still-rules

Innovate your recruitment

If you are recruiting people you want to be innovative you are under some scrutiny to lead by example. The kind of people who will disrupt your firm from the inside won't necessarily tick the boxes of a traditional person specification. Can you innovate your recruitment process and try a different approach? Where are the real edgy innovators hanging out? Probably not in the job section of *The Guardian*.

Case study

The Cystic Fibrosis Trust

The Cystic Fibrosis Trust in the UK took a different approach when recruiting a Director of Engagement. The post was advertised as a Master Storyteller, whose job it was to engage with a number of audiences. Rather than the conventional CV candidates were asked to make a two-minute video about the day that Cystic Fibrosis was beaten for good. It was a successful new approach and the provocative question really made the candidates focus on the purpose of the role they were applying for.

Whether you are recruiting a separate innovation team or innovators into every team, consider the following qualities:

- **Attitude over experience:** the person who isn't afraid to admit that they don't know the answer to a problem but can work with others to find it. A person who focuses on the reasons that something can be done, rather than the reasons why it can't.
- **Flexibility:** they can think on their feet and are adaptable to change. They are able to throw away their old plans and make new ones that better suit the changing situation.
- **Resilient:** they are pragmatic, they understand that not everyone will like an idea and they don't take it personally. They

have strength to admit to failures, learn and adapt. They don't take no for an answer.

- **Strategic:** they are able to think strategically and see the long-term big picture and keep focused on the purpose of innovation.
- **Curious and inquisitive:** they ask questions to understand situations and are collectors and sharers of ideas and raw material for innovation.
- **Exceptional communicators:** they are able to adapt to different communication styles to suit their audiences' preferences and have a natural talent to enthuse and influence.
- **Good listeners:** they take time and enjoy really listening and understanding others, they are accepting and not judging others' points of view.
- **Self-starters:** they are motivated to keep moving forward even when there are obstacles, they are good lateral thinkers and are able to find solutions to problems.
- **Team workers:** they work well with others and support the team to achieve shared goals.
- **Collaborative:** they work with other people and are skilled at identifying and finding win–win propositions to get partners on board.
- **Excellent network builders:** both of existing networks and they restlessly look for opportunities to make connections across a range of industries and sectors.
- **Humble:** they can put their ego to one side and are not afraid to show vulnerability and ask for help.
- **Entrepreneurial spirit:** they are able to spot opportunities that make good financial business sense.

Get the mix right

Overall it is the value of the mix of diverse skills, experience, passion and personalities that spark ideas off each other that creates innovation magic. That's what you are looking for. And you will know when you have got it. Good luck.

Checklist

- Recruit based on entrepreneurial attitude over experience.
- Look for differences in skills and experiences.
- Lead by example.

Reading a book to improve your innovation skills is the first step on a bigger journey to innovation excellence. One tried and tested way to improve your skills over time is to work with a mentor, someone you trust, with relevant experience in the areas you wish to improve on, who works with you over a defined timescale to achieve specific goals. This section will help you to find and work with a mentor.

Post self-assessment

Take the questionnaire **on page 205.** Which areas have developed and which still require attention? Perhaps there are some parts of the innovation process that are simply not relevant to you, but others that are very much part of your day-to-day work that would benefit from development. Take a moment to reflect and write down:

- What have you learned?
- What can you take forward now?
- In which areas would you like to improve your skills?

Based on your questionnaire answers and the steps in the book you may find it helpful to note your needs on an innovation skills matrix. Plot on the next page where you are on a scale of 1–10, with 1 being little or no skills in that specific area and 10 being an expert. Think about the areas where you would like to make improvements. Innovation is a big topic that requires multiple skills. Don't feel that you have to be expert at every area, but consider the areas that have most interest and relevance to you and start with those.

Skill	Current	Desired	Goals
Identify problems			
Understand customers			
Market insight			
Creative capacity			
Idea generation			
Influencing			
Filter and choose ideas			
Prototype, fail and refine			
Pilot, adapt and invest			
Take to market			

A guide to using your skills in action with your mentor

The skills and ideas in this book will take time to develop. We learn by doing, not by reading theory. While some of the tips may act as quick fixes, to truly master the techniques and make them an automatic feature of your work you will need to apply the theory to your everyday life, revisit the exercises and keep up to date with your customers, the marketplace and new innovations on a regular basis.

Achieving lasting change requires work and dedication, which can, when the workload is stacking up, be difficult to maintain.

One of the best ways of ensuring that you continue to develop and hone your innovation skills, guaranteeing that this book has a lasting positive impact, is to work with a mentor: someone who can support your development, challenge you, ensure you continue to apply your learning and make progress.

Finding a mentor

A mentor could be a colleague, manager or someone from outside your organisation with relevant experience who has an interest in helping you to develop. When identifying potential mentors, think about the areas that you have identified that you would like to work on and consider:

- Who demonstrates the skills that you wish to perfect?
- Who is where you would like to be in one, five or ten years' time?
- Who has a track record in delivering innovation projects?
- Who has turned their career opportunities into successes?
- Who is working for an organisation that you aspire to be an employee of?

It also needs to be a win–win situation so consider what would be in it for them. There can be great satisfaction in helping another person, and for some, being an innovation mentor would help develop their coaching skills which can in turn help their own development. Alternatively, they might even be looking for a new innovation recruit.

Approaching a mentor

You might already know the person you would like to mentor you. Or you might have to practise your networking skills and be introduced to them. It is important to find someone you trust, and that you have rapport with, so the first step is to have an initial meeting to:

- explain what you are looking for;
- check the person has the same understanding and is happy to be a mentor;
- establish that you have trust and rapport (particularly if you do not already know the person);
- agree that you are both comfortable to proceed.

Working with your mentor

It is your responsibility to agree with your mentor how you will work together, how long the relationship will last as well as your goals. Together with your mentor agree the following:

- **How often you meet**: this depends on what you are working on and what you want to achieve and the time that your mentor has available. A workable timescale is every six weeks, enough time to complete activities discussed in the meeting, and close enough together to keep momentum.

- **Where to meet**: I recommend going somewhere away from your usual workplace where you can feel relaxed and are able to speak freely.

- **How long your meetings will be**: again it depends on what works for both you and your mentor but 90 minutes is a good chunk of time to discuss several topics, set goals and reflect on progress without feeling rushed.

- **Time of day**: often first thing in the morning or over lunch works well and has minimum impact on your own and your mentor's day-to-day work.

- **How long the relationship will last**: a typical mentoring relationship lasts for a year, but depending on your needs it could last a shorter or longer time. The important thing is to agree together how long it will last.

- **Your goals**: what do you want to achieve through the mentoring relationship? Use the matrix and questionnaire as a starting point and set SMART goals together.

- **Support**: outside of the mentoring meetings what support are they able to give you. For example, can you call them if you need urgent advice on an innovation project, or advice on a business case that might not wait until the next meeting?

- **Confidentiality**: agree if your meetings are to be confidential, especially important if you are discussing new projects or ways to influence colleagues which could be sensitive.

It's helpful to keep a written record of what you agree for reference on both sides to ensure you both have the same understanding and expectations of the relationship.

Structure your meetings

It is helpful to structure your meetings to ensure that you spend time on:

- setting and revising your goals;
- personal reflection on your progress;
- skill development around specific agreed areas;
- actions.

Using the post-assessment questionnaire and the skills matrix, set some goals with your mentor. For example, you might consider where you want to be in five years' time, or you may want to focus on more immediate goals like moving a specific project to the next stage. Pick a timescale that feels right for you: for some people five years is too far off, for others, it's too soon. If you know what your end goal is, then you can work out the steps you need to take and the skills you need to develop to get you there. You can work with your mentor to think about your big picture goal: for example, do you want to be Head of Innovation by the time you are 35? To lead an innovation team you need management skills, to have a track record of taking products to market and be able to make quick strategic decisions. What are the small steps you need to take to get there, and by when? Spend time at every meeting checking in on progress against goals and adjusting them as necessary as you progress.

Personal reflection

Allocate some time with your mentor for personal reflection. Time spent reflecting on your progress and noting your achievements will help to build your confidence. Understanding workplace experiences and relationships also helps to develop your self-awareness. Working with a mentor from outside of your immediate team can help to challenge your assumptions and work through different scenarios to help build resilience, problem solve and improve your ability to work with others in specific situations.

You may discover:

- that you are making great progress;
- helpful/unhelpful patterns of behaviour;
- hidden motivators;
- strengths/areas for development;
- causes of anxiety;
- sources of energy/enthusiasm/interest.

Skill development

To be a good innovator you need a broad range of skills including problem solving, creative thinking, research, analysis, strategy, influencing and project management. You will not be equally strong in all areas. Use the questionnaire and work with your mentor to work on the specific skills that you want to develop as part of your goal setting. Remember that innovation requires a varied skills set and you may choose to focus on one or two areas that you are most interested in or that are most relevant to your current or desired next role. Don't put yourself under pressure to excel at everything. That said, you are accountable for your own development and part of your mentor's role is to agree your areas for goals and not let you off the hook, in order that you achieve them.

Actions

Agree specific actions at the end of each meeting, for which you are accountable, and that you report back on them at your next meeting. It is also helpful to keep a log to record your progress between meetings that you can use to reflect and ensure that all relevant issues are discussed. It is easy if, for example, you are meeting at six-weekly intervals to forget some of your achievements. The purpose of your mentor relationship is to push your development and being aware of, and recording your progress is a key part of that.

And finally

Enjoy yourself!

You should now have a good understanding of what innovation is, a sense of the skills that you are already accomplished in, clarity on the areas that you want to develop and a plan to help you do it.

Remember that innovation is not something that should just be confined to your day-to-day work environment; you can apply the skills to every aspect of your life. Learning to solve problems, exploring creative solutions that you can then put into action can reap rewards and help you achieve your ambitions both professionally and personally. Innovation presents a world of possibilities and the only way you make those possibilities happen is by taking action. The more effort you put in, the bigger the rewards that you will get back. Start right now, tackle innovation head on – and blaze a trail.

Self-assessment questionnaire

Once you have read the book or the parts of the book that are relevant to your needs and completed the exercises, complete the questionnaire again. Score yourself 1–10 for each of the questions. 10 indicates a high level of confidence and skill and 1 a low level.

Don't think too hard about your answers. There is no right answer. Complete it quickly using your gut instinct.

1. I am confident at identifying the root cause of a problem.

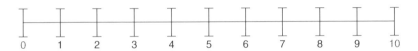

2. I am creative.

3. I can easily come up with multiple solutions to problems.

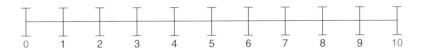

4. I am excellent at making my ideas happen.

5. I have large and diverse networks.

6. I know how to develop my ideas.

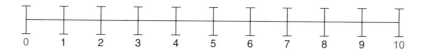

7. I can easily decide where to focus to make the most difference.

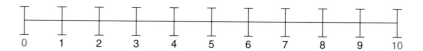

8. I am quick to spot potential new opportunities.

9. I am flexible to adapt or change my plans if situations change.

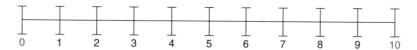

10. I have a good understanding of my customers and the marketplace.

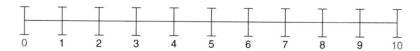

11. I am comfortable to challenge the status quo.

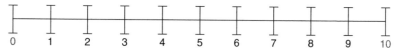

12. I regularly step outside my comfort zone and try new things.

13. I happily admit my mistakes in order that I, and others learn from them.

14. I am comfortable asking others for help and advice.

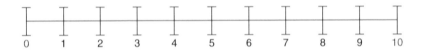

15. I am a great listener.

16. I feel equipped to influence and inspire others to get on board with my ideas.

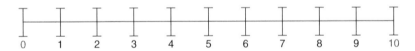

17. I am confident in developing strategic business models.

18. I am objective in making strategic decisions about both progressing and stopping ideas.

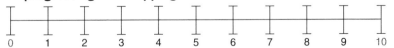

19. I do what I believe to be right, even if others criticise me for it.

0   1   2   3   4   5   6   7   8   9   10

20. I am willing to take risks and go the extra mile to achieve better results.

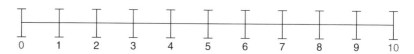

0   1   2   3   4   5   6   7   8   9   10

- **Angel investor:** also known as a business angel, an affluent individual who provides capital for a business startup, usually in exchange for convertible debt or ownership equity.
- **Audience:** a group of people reached by an activity.
- **BAU:** Business As Usual – the normal execution of operations within an organisation.
- **Bodystorming:** a technique used in interaction design or to stimulate creativity. The idea is to imagine what it would be like if the product existed, and act as though it exists, ideally in the place it would be used.
- **Brainstorming:** holding a group discussion to produce ideas.
- **Brand positioning:** the place in the consumer's mind that you want your brand to own.
- **Burning platform:** a crisis, either natural or engineered to force change.
- **Business angel:** see 'Angel investor'.
- **Business case:** captures the reasoning for initiating an idea, project or task.
- **Business model:** a plan for the successful operation of a business, identifying sources of revenue, the intended customer base, products and details of financing.
- **Categories:** classes or divisions of people or products that have shared characteristics.
- **Challenge prize:** a way to accelerate change by offering a reward to whoever can first, or most effectively, meet a defined challenge.
- **Co-creation:** a strategy that brings together different groups to jointly produce a mutually valued outcome.

- **Collaboration:** the action of working with others to produce something.
- **Comfort zone:** a psychological state in which a person feels familiar, at ease, in control and experiences low anxiety to deliver a typically steady level of performance with little or no risk.
- **Competence:** the ability to do something successfully or efficiently.
- **Concept:** an abstract idea, an invention, a plan or intention.
- **Confident:** feeling or showing certainty about something, for example, oneself or one's abilities or qualities.
- **Consumer:** a person who purchases goods and services or eats or uses something.
- **Corporate Social Responsibility:** CSR is a strategy whereby companies integrate social and environmental concerns in their business operations.
- **Creativity:** the ability to generate or recognise ideas, alternatives or possibilities.
- **Crowd:** a group of people gathered together; or a group of people united by a common characteristic.
- **Crowdfund:** raising money to fund a project or venture from a large number of people, typically via the internet.
- **Crowdsource:** gaining information or input into a task or project by enlisting the services of a number of people, either paid or unpaid, typically via the internet.
- **Culture:** the ideas, customs and social behaviour of a particular people or society, or 'how we do things here'.
- **Customer:** a person or group of people who receives or consumes products and has the ability to choose between different products and suppliers.
- **Customer segment:** the act of separating customers into groups defined by their characteristics, for example age, gender, demographic, buying behaviours, etc.

- **Design thinking:** a process of creating new ideas and solving problems using visual methods combined with data to provide value for customers.
- **Disruptive innovation:** a new process, product or service that displaces or disrupts an existing market.
- **Early adopter:** a person who embraces new technology, products or services before most other people do.
- **Ethnography:** rooted in anthropology, ethnography is the discipline and systematic study of people and cultures by spending quality time with the group of people one is interested in.
- **Fad:** any form of behaviour that develops among a large population, is perceived as 'cool' and is collectively followed enthusiastically for a period of time.
- **Feedback sandwich:** giving someone a piece of positive feedback, followed by negative feedback and then a piece of positive feedback.
- **Frugal innovation:** making high-quality products from limited resources.
- **Fuzzy front end:** typically experimental activities and research that occur before the formal and well-defined new-product development process.
- **Game changing:** having the potential to significantly change the outcome of something.
- **Gamification:** the application of elements of game playing, e.g. point scoring and competition with others, to other areas of activity. Typically used as an online marketing technique to encourage engagement with a product or service.
- **GeoVation:** innovation around a challenge that involves geographical data as a key component.
- **Hack or hack day:** gathering a group of experts, typically involving programmers and others involved in software development, to solve problems or build something quickly.
- **Icebreaker:** a game or activity that is used to introduce people to each other so that they feel more relaxed together.

- **Imitation:** simulating or copying something else.
- **Improvise:** create and perform spontaneously or without preparation, or to produce and make something from whatever is available.
- **Incremental innovation:** making small improvements to an existing product, process or service.
- **Innovation:** the action or process of innovating; a new method, idea, product or service.
- **Insight:** the capacity to gain an accurate and deep understanding of someone or something.
- **Key Performance Indicator:** a KPI is a type of performance measurement that evaluates the success of an organisation, individual or particular activity in which they engage.
- **Lean startup:** a method for developing businesses and products based on a build–measure–learn feedback loop, first proposed by Eric Ries in 2011.
- **Live environment:** working in a real market environment for product testing, rather than a focus group or simulated environment.
- **Managing-up:** to build a successful relationship with a superior, manager or employer.
- **Market segment:** to divide a broad market into subsets, for example consumers or businesses which have common needs and priorities and designing and implementing strategies to target them.
- **Mentor:** an experienced and trusted advisor.
- **Metric:** a system or standard of measurement.
- **Minimum viable product:** MVP is a term used in product development and lean startup methodology. It refers to the minimum sufficient features to satisfy early adopters of a product, and provides a feedback loop to guide future development.
- **Motivation:** the desire to do things.
- **Netnography:** the branch of ethnography that analyses the free behaviour of individuals on the internet which uses online marketing research techniques to provide useful insights.

- **Niche market:** the typically small and particular subset of a market segment on which a specific product is focused.
- **Niche product:** a product or service with features that appeal to a very particular market segment.
- **Open innovation:** innovating with individuals and companies from outside your organisation and sharing the risks and rewards.
- **Opportunity cost:** a benefit, profit or value of something that must be given up to acquire or achieve something else. Everything (time, money, skills) can be put to alternative uses; every action therefore has an associated opportunity cost.
- **Patent:** limited legal monopoly granted to an individual or firm to make, use and sell its invention and to exclude others from doing so.
- **Phase gate:** see Stage gate.
- **Product:** anything that can be offered to a market or consumer that might satisfy a want or need.
- **Project management:** the application of processes, methods, knowledge, skills and experience to achieve the project objectives.
- **Proposition:** a proposal; a subject for discussion or analysis; a plan suggested for acceptance.
- **Prototype:** an early sample, model or release of a product to test a concept or process or to act as a thing to be replicated or learned from.
- **Purpose:** the reason for which something is done or created or for which something exists.
- **Radical innovation:** an innovation that has a significant impact on a market.
- **Research and development:** R&D is a systematic activity directed towards innovation; the introduction and improvement of products, services and processes.
- **Scale:** refers to the size of the business, or the optimisation of the business to drive the greatest volume and results.
- **Shelf life:** the length of time that a product or idea can exist without becoming unfit for consumption, or irrelevant.

- **Skunkworks:** a small group of people who work on a project in a typically unconventional way to develop something quickly and with minimal management constraints.
- **SMART objectives:** are Simple, Measurable, Achievable, Realistic and Time specific.
- **Social capital:** the networks of relationships among people who live and work in a particular society, enabling that society to function effectively.
- **Social enterprise:** a business that exists to tackle social problems, reinvesting its profits into the business.
- **Social value:** a measure of an organisation's or individual's contribution to society, including the impact on the wellbeing of individuals and communities, social capital and the environment.
- **Solution:** a means of solving a problem or dealing with a difficult situation.
- **Sphere of activity and influence:** the individuals and groups that one works with, or whose work impacts and influences.
- **Stage gate:** part of an innovation or new product development process. Each stage of development is separated by 'gates', each gate being a point of sign-off before proceeding to the next stage.
- **Stakeholder:** a person with an interest or concern in something, especially business.
- **Stuck:** baffled or nonplussed, caught or fixed.
- **Take to market:** a set of integrated tactics to connect with customers.
- **Team:** a group that comes together to achieve a common goal.
- **Unmet need:** a need of an individual or group that is not being met; which could be with or without their knowledge.
- **Workshop:** a meeting at which a group of people engage in intensive discussion and activity on a particular subject or project.

Lateral thinking answers

These are the actual answers to the activities. There are many solutions to the same problem. Did you come up with something even better?

Shoe shop shuffle

The shoe shops put single shoes as display items outside the shops. One shop puts left shoes on display, the other three shops put right shoes. Thieves stole the display shoes, but had to make pairs, so more shoes were taken from the one displaying left shoes. The manager changed the display to right shoes and thefts dropped significantly.

School inspector

Before the school inspector arrived, the teacher instructed the pupils always to raise their left hands if they did not know the answer or were unsure. If they were sure they knew the answer they should raise their right hand. The teacher chose a different person every time, but always one who had raised his or her right hand. The inspector was duly impressed.

Wrong number

The marketing manager called the telephone company that issued numbers and bought the wrong number. The line was redirected to the call centre and the mailing was sent out.

Price tag

The practice originated to ensure that the clerk had to open the till and give change for each transaction. This recorded the sale and prevented the clerk from pocketing the money.

Answer to innovator's dilemma

Here's the subtle difference. This attractive alternative project has two stages. The first is a pilot, costing £1,000. The pilot has a 90 per cent chance of failing, which would end the whole project. If the pilot succeeds, scaling up will cost a further £10,000, and there will be a 10 per cent chance of a million-pound payday.

This two-stage structure changes everything. While the total cost is still £11,000 and the chance of success is still 1 per cent, the option to get out after a failed pilot is invaluable. Nine times out of ten, the pilot will save you from wasting £10,000 – which means that while the simple project offers an expected loss of £1,000, the two-stage project has an expected profit of £8,000.

Answer to the nine dots puzzle

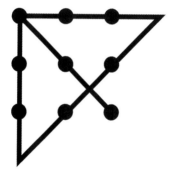

Sometimes you have to think outside the box.

What did you think of this book?

We're really keen to hear from you about this book, so that we can make our publishing even better.

Please log on to the following website and leave us your feedback.

It will only take a few minutes and your thoughts are invaluable to us.

www.pearsoned.co.uk/bookfeedback

Do you want your people to be the very best at what they do?

Talk to us about how we can help.

As the world's leading learning company, we know a lot about what your people need in order to be better at what they do.

Whatever subject or skills you've got in mind (from presenting or persuasion to coaching or communication skills), and at whatever level (from new-starters through to top executives) we can help you deliver tried-and-tested, essential learning straight to your workforce – whatever they need, whenever they need it and wherever they are.

Talk to us today about how we can:

- Complement and support your existing learning and development programmes
- Enhance and augment your people's learning experience
- Match your needs to the best of our content
- Customise, brand and change it to make a better fit
- Deliver cost-effective, great value learning content that's proven to work.

Contact us today:
corporate.enquiries@pearson.com